Country Creations:
Woodworking Projects to Make and Sell

Country Creations: Woodworking Projects to Make and Sell

James E. Seitz
Linda S. Yaklich

TAB BOOKS
Blue Ridge Summit, PA

FIRST EDITION
FIRST PRINTING

© 1991 by **TAB Books**.
TAB Books is a division of McGraw-Hill, Inc.

Library of Congress Cataloging-in-Publication Data

Seitz, James E.
   Country creations : woodworking projects to make and sell / by
James E. Seitz and Linda S. Yaklich.
     p.   cm.
   Includes index.
   ISBN 0-8306-2144-X (pbk.)
   1. Woodwork. I. Yaklich, Linda S. II. Title.
TT180.S397 1991
684′.08—dc20   91-20566
                                             CIP

Acquisitions Editor: Kimberly Tabor
Book Editor: April D. Nolan
Page Makeup: Toya B. Warner
Production: Katherine G. Brown
Book Design: Jaclyn J. Boone
Color photography by Susan Riley, Harrisonburg, VA
Special thanks to Robin and Grayson Newberry
for their help with color photographs.

To those who nostalgically ponder,
as we occasionally do,
the once familiar manner of country living.

Contents

Projects ix

Acknowledgments xi

Introduction xiii

1 The Country Style 1
An American Tradition 1
A Handy Homecraft 2
Decorative Design 3
Practical Purposes 5
Developing Designs 5

2 Constructing and Coloring 7
Preparing Patterns 7
Tools and Materials 8
Hooks and Hangers 12
Lettering and Stenciling 14
Painting and Staining 15

3 Colorful Cutouts 18
Forming Flat Figures 18

4 Miniatures and Magnets 31
Mini Making 31
Attaching Magnets, Clasps, and Cords 32

5 Attractive Assemblies   **42**

Shaping and Assembling   42

6 Mottos and Messages   **52**

Sample Slogans   52
Forms   54
Lettering by Stenciling   55

7 Comical Creations   **64**

Creating Comical Characters   64

8 Household Holders   **79**

Fashioning Functional Forms   79

9 Shelves, Seats, and Stools   **90**

Practical Processes   90

10 Making It Pay   **101**

The Home Advantage   101
Practical Procedures   102
Supplying the Skills   102
Pricing and Promoting   103
Having a Party   105
Taking Orders and Keeping Track   107

Index   **109**

Projects

COLORFUL CUTOUTS

Hung-Up Horse ... *20*
Close Couples and Solemn Singles ... *22*
Basket Bearer ... *26*
Amish Couples ... *29*

MINIATURES AND MAGNETS

Fashionable Figures ... *34*
Delightful Decorations ... *36*
Bears, Bunnies, and Buildings ... *38*

ATTRACTIVE ASSEMBLIES

Colorful Weathercock ... *44*
Duck by Candlelight ... *47*
Big-Eared Bunnies ... *49*

MOTTOS AND MESSAGES

A Country Welcome ... *56*
Heartfelt Hello ... *58*
Rowdy Roosters ... *59*

COMICAL CREATIONS

"You Do It" ... *67*
Munching Mouse ... *70*

Fat Cat   73
Homey Humor   74

HOUSEHOLD HOLDERS

Decorative Towel Dispenser   82
Modern Matchbox   83
Kitty Cat Bookrack   87

SHELVES, SEATS, AND STOOLS

Shaker-Peg Shelf   91
Sturdy Step Stool   95
Sulker's Seat   97

Acknowledgments

Besides being the one principally involved in the construction and marketing of wooden country figures, co-author Linda Yaklich deserves recognition for having developed the profitable business which inspired this writing. Her young children—Uriah, Jackson, and Rachael—sometimes lent a much appreciated, helping hand. Their assistance took the form of occasionally sanding cutouts in the shop or doing chores about the homestead, although many of the pieces shown in the text are Linda's creations entirely.

Credit for the writing, illustrating, photography, and some of the projects and designs goes to Linda's father and co-author, James Seitz. He, in turn, credits Arlene, his wife, for many of the photographs. Additional expressions of appreciation are extended to the editorial staff for their assistance and to the several owners of Linda's creations who made certain pieces available for photographing.

James E. Seitz, Ph.D.
and Linda S. Yaklich

Introduction

If you are interested in fashioning articles in the country style, whether you are a beginner or a highly skilled craftsman, you can profit from this book. It contains easy-to-use drawings and instructions for making wooden articles of marketable quality, and the many patterns included are graded to challenge both the experienced practitioner and the novice. While the book has primarily a project orientation, it also contains explanations on how to design in the country style and how to successfully sell the articles. These explanations and all other aspects of the book are based on our own experiences.

The text contains complete descriptions of projects, many of which are new variations of familiar subjects. We have included numerous patterns in a variety of decorative and functional designs. Each pattern is accompanied by a photograph of the completed project, a list of the tools and material required, descriptions (with drawings and photographs) of special points to observe in the shop, and other supplementary information of historical or practical nature. We've included both traditional Early American projects as well as projects in a contemporary form of folk art which has recently surged in popularity. Our suggestions for decorating the different pieces should encourage you to apply your own special touch.

The methods of construction are intentionally basic. Although the sizes range from about an inch across to a five-foot length, many of the projects are of single-board thickness and can be cut from a small section of 1 × 8. Several of the larger items do require assembling with pegs and screws, but all projects were designed with ease of construction in mind.

From a beginning explanation of the meaning and purpose of country styling, the text moves quickly into the project themes that make up the bulk of the work, including plain folks, farm figures, miniatures, magnets, built-up beauties, comical creations, mottos, household holders, stools, and shelves. Many chapters contain helpful examples of how to be creative yet true to style, and all of them bring together the kinds of details needed by those who want ready-made patterns, as well as suggestions for the more advanced craftsmen who want to make designs of their own.

The final chapter, which provides you with the techniques for marketing the products at a profit, is an added bonus. We have covered only those practices that have produced significant results for us in our communities, but skillful application of the principles and methods used should prove equally successful in other parts of the country.

1

The Country Style

The country style of decoration has distinctive and appealing qualities. It is essentially a product of rural inspiration and has the generally pleasant characteristics of a home craft. It might be rustic, quaint, or homey, given a traditional treatment or a relatively modern flavor. Regardless, this particular form of folk art seems to satisfy a nostalgic appeal for the charm of things once common throughout the countryside. Perhaps that feeling, more than anything else, is the reason for the style's prolonged popularity.

One-room school desks, farm buildings, barnyard animals, and all sorts of teddy bears and rabbits—some stenciled and some painted freehand—are among the many different items built to reduced size to help retain memories of one's past. On the other hand, certain pieces are seldom down-sized or given a contemporary characteristic. For example, copies of Early American utensils and furniture are often made as exact and as functional as the original creations.

AN AMERICAN TRADITION

Before the late nineteenth century, handcrafting by ordinary people was commonplace in America, but this practice eventually gave way to the increasingly widespread use of machines. By the turn of the century, mechanical devices had displaced the work done entirely on an individual basis, except for what continued in isolated areas. Changing tastes and the economy of mass production pushed the need for the piece-by-piece wooden creations of both skilled and unskilled folks into virtual obscurity. No longer was there a pronounced demand for the carved figureheads of ships, wooden grave markers, cigar-store indians, decoys, weathervanes, butter molds, and handcrafted toys.

It was not until about 1920 that the demand for folk art and crafts again emerged. The fresh, simple properties of the creations and the absence of concern for the formal rules of art and construction accounted for much of the appeal developing beyond the confines of the museums. The handmade artifacts became highly prized for what they reveal about early life, but they were mainly crafted in an untutored, primitive manner. However, recent adaptations of wooden crafts have developed to fulfill a personal desire for peaceful alternatives to the hubbub of modern life. Things related to nature, an unpretentious representation of mundane subjects, a display of sentimental, religious, or proverbial wisdom, and an obvious quality of being homemade account for much of the interest in the craft today.

That the demand for country creations in wood continues is undoubtedly certain. The growth of cottage industries in recent years is one bit of evidence; another is the development of an entire chain of retail outlets and sections of variety stores throughout the nation as a source for paints and accessories for making items in the manner of folk art.

For the most part, the work today centers on aspects of country art in the general sense. Substyles, such as the specialized forms developed by the Shakers and the Pennsylvania Dutch (actually German settlers), currently occupy craftsmen's attention in lesser proportions. Their value as noteworthy crafts remains important, nonetheless.

A HANDY HOMECRAFT

One of the practical values of designing and building in the country manner is its comparative ease. The work can be done with a few tools and minimal effort, for it doesn't need the highly polished finishing touches modern pieces require. In fact, rough textures, dull surfaces, and simple joinery are the desired effects in country styling.

As with the work done historically, many things of practical worth can be made and applied directly in the home. Figure 1-1 illustrates stenciling and woodwork that comply with the country style of design. The wall paintings include the traditional tree of life, and the shelf contains the commonly used cutout of hearts. The wood's rustic appearance complements the idea of antiquity of design and application.

***Fig. 1-1.** Stenciled walls, antique lace, shaker pegs, heart designs, dipped candles, and rustic woodwork—all contribute effectively to a traditional country decor.*

You can do much of the work for these projects by hand, just as it was done in a previous era, but for convenience's sake, we recommend you use labor-saving tools whenever feasible. Their use effectively simplifies the work without diminishing or detracting from the style. Power tools can produce an end product that captures all of the simple beauty and charm of an original—and at a far reduced investment of time.

DECORATIVE DESIGN

Decoration constitutes a major purpose of country art. Pieces made from wood for hanging to the wall or for standing on a shelf are almost always intended to be decorative—whether they are finished in the "natural," painted freehand in multicolored tones, or adorned with stenciled figures. Such pieces are meant to carry some attraction for the viewer, which can vary from the simple likeness of a cute or cuddly creature to the representation of something that has acquired a symbolic meaning.

Objects made for a dual purpose, that is for both a decorative and a symbolic effect, are commonplace in homes furnished in the country style. Beautifully decorated signs and plaques that carry meaningful messages in stenciled letters are an example. More specifically, the use of hearts and doves in artistic arrangements on boards that bear statements of greeting convey to the visitor not just a simple "welcome," but a welcome in a loving way.

Figure 1-2 represents a scene of probable occurrence in years past, an old-fashioned spring cleaning. The presence of geese (though not exactly naturalistic) places the chore in the country, and the use of patterns of hearts and calico further contribute to the style. The effect of flat (nonglossy) paints throughout also adds a sense of antiquity to the display.

Fig. 1-2. *This decorative piece, crafted in popular country style, brings back memories of a once-familiar scene.*

PRACTICAL PURPOSES

Country creations do not have to be pieces that are viewed and adored but nothing else. In fact, they can easily be designed to perform some useful function. Tables, benches, stools, shelves, and the like are examples of such practical projects. Any decorative effect these things have is secondary to their function.

This is not to say that functional pieces have no artistic appeal. Usually the very opposite is often true, as a weathervane illustrates. Traditionally, a crowing cock was fashioned and placed on the weather arrow so that it would present some attraction while pointing in the direction of the wind. A rectangular block of wood might have functioned as well, but it would not have been as artistic.

In many instances, the elements of art do not stand out so vividly. Some of the utensils passed down from colonial days fill that category. The scoops, dippers, troughs, and trays that served such useful purposes in the home derive what beauty they have from their shapes. Form alone can determine a piece's artistic value. Indeed, many items are collected today for their appearance rather than for their useful application.

DEVELOPING DESIGNS

The designs in the chapters that follow are made for duplicating essentially as they are presented, but we urge those who want to broaden their skills to experiment with various alternatives. A good way to begin is to alter the colors. After that, attempt subtle changes in shapes until you can create pieces that are entirely your own. Throughout the text, we provide you with instructions that will help you to develop the necessary skills.

Some designs, such as the decorative piece in FIG. 1-3, are much more advanced than others in complexity of construction. A beginner might want to simplify such designs, perhaps by leaving the edges of the different parts unrounded, or by making the figure from one flat board and painting in most of the details. In this manner, you can alter many of the patterns that follow to suit your ability and taste.

Fig. 1-3. Country figures of modern design, such as this big-eared bunny, are often adorned with calico ribbon.

It is important to note that merely changing size does not constitute redesigning. The useful technique of enlarging or reducing a pattern's dimensions overall changes nothing but size. Whether you make the change with the method of squares (explained in chapter 2) or by photocopying makes no substantial difference. The object's shape, proportions, and style remain as originally designed. With this in mind, you might find it helpful to enlarge the patterns to the dimensions of the original pieces (as given in the material lists).

The designs presented are appropriate for most ordinary purposes. Because many are based on the experience of successful selling, you might not want to alter them at all. However, if a client asks for some custom-made piece, an ability to create an original will come in handy, so don't overlook the procedures and instructions for work of that kind.

2

Constructing
and Coloring

The procedures for making and finishing country creations in wood are comparatively simple. For one thing, the designs are not very complicated. Many articles are made from a single piece, and the assemblies involve only the simplest methods of joinery. A saw, drill, and hammer are the principal tools needed for cutting and assembling.

Finishing, too, has the advantage of simplicity. Country articles often require only uniformly flat coatings. Acrylics are ideal because they are naturally dull when dry. Even when the detailing requires some skill in handling fine brushes, you won't need to master the kind of shading you see in an artist's oil paintings. Country decorating becomes even easier with the use of stencils to guide the painting of figures and letters (FIG. 2-1).

PREPARING PATTERNS

The outline drawings in the chapters that follow may be used as they are or altered to suit your own needs. Many of the patterns are intended for enlarging on paper to fit the materials listed and for tracing onto the wood itself. Alternately, you can pencil-trace the shapes onto a cardboard template. If you want to change the size of a given design, you can use either the method of squares or photographic reduction or enlargement. While photocopiers sometimes produce superior results, they are not a convenient or cost-effective means for people who don't have access to their own copier.

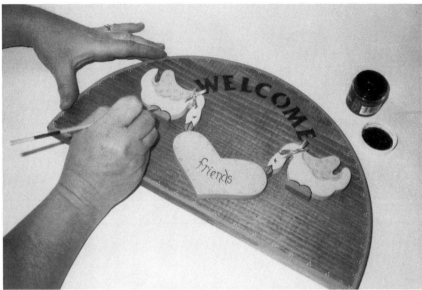

Fig. 2-1. *Simple construction and the use of flat paints and stains characterize country art in wood.*

To use the method of squares, first draw squares of equal size (about 1 inch) across the pattern as presented; then on a second sheet construct squares of larger or smaller size as desired. Now draw shapes within each square on the second sheet comparable to those on the original. Notice, in particular, where the figure's outline intersects each line of the squares. Figure 2-2 shows an enlargement in progress.

Once you have completed a drawing, transfer the outline onto the wood using tracing paper (FIG. 2-3), or make a cardboard template. Keep in mind that a template comes in handy if you're making multiple pieces of the same shape (FIG. 2-4).

TOOLS AND MATERIALS

The processes of shaping, assembling, and finishing tend to determine what tools you need. The first of these, shaping, utilizes devices for sawing and sanding.

Although you can complete much of the work with hand saws, we recommend using a power saw for virtually all the initial shaping. A circular saw is useful for squaring and beveling; a band saw or jigsaw (FIG. 2-5) for cutting irregular figures from thick stock; and a scroll saw for cutting along the edges of small shapes outlined on the thinner woods. A hand-held jigsaw will do just about everything the other saws will do, but don't overlook the convenience of a scroll saw for the fine work.

Fig. 2-2. The method of squares allows you to draw a larger pattern of a given shape.

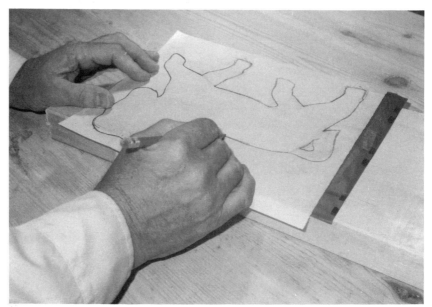

Fig. 2-3. Transfer the enlargement to the wood using a blunt pencil and carbon paper.

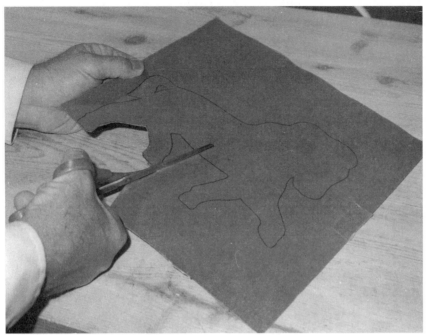

Fig. 2-4. *Producing a cardboard template of the enlargement is an alternate means of tracing the outline onto the wood.*

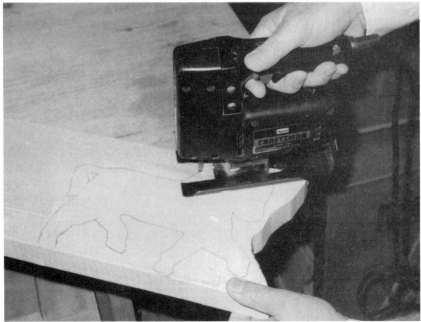

Fig. 2-5. *A jigsaw is particularly useful for cutting out shapes from thick stock.*

The final shaping of a cutout involves the rounding of edges and the smoothing of surfaces. You can do much of the work by hand with a piece of graded sandpaper wrapped around a block of wood. Although they are not completely essential, power-driven drum, disk, and orbital sanders are effective timesavers (FIG. 2-6), as are the hand rasp and power router for rounding edges.

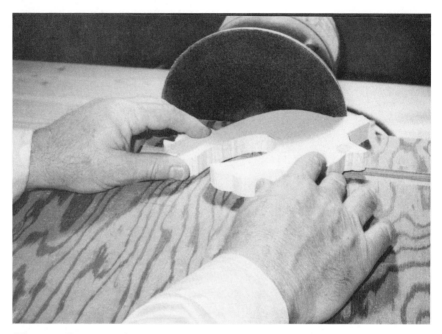

Fig. 2-6. Power-sanding can alleviate much of the drudgery of sanding rough edges by hand.

The assembling stage also requires few power tools. In fact, a drill is the only electrical device we recommend for this purpose; either a portable or stationary drill will do the job. The hand tools you'll need at different times include wood clamps, a screwdriver, and a hammer and nail set.

You need brushes of various kinds for finishing, except when applying a clear sealer from a spray can. Use flat brushes in widths up to an inch for applying acrylics and polyurethane over large areas and small, flat, and pointed artist's brushes for detailing in different colors. Water and mineral spirits, respectively, are the solvents for cleaning brushes used in applying the acrylics and polyurethane.

As to the choice of wood, most articles can be made out of 1 × 8 softwood. Clear spruce or pine serves very well, but lower grades will do if you cut around the knots and imperfections. For the thick pieces, softwood of a nominal 2-inch thickness and widths of 4, 6, or 8 inches will be adequate for most purposes.

Multi-piece creations are assembled using sections of dowel rods of different diameters and woodworking glue. A quick-setting adhesive helps you avoid long periods of delay in construction. Wood screws and brads are preferable to dowels and glue for some applications.

When you review the lists of material and tools for each project, be aware that alternatives will often do just as well. The items and dimensions of lumber listed represent the things we used in constructing the originals. Any change in the sizes of the patterns might make the width and length measurements invalid to some extent. For ordinary applications, however, such differences will probably be inconsequential.

HOOKS AND HANGERS

You can buy hangers in several different shapes and sizes, but the sawtooth forms are the most useful for hanging wooden cutouts. You can easily attach these to the back of an article with small wire nails (FIG. 2-7).

The problem with saw-tooth hangers, as with other metal hangers, is that the pieces to which they are attached cannot fit flat against the wall. A gap occurs regardless of the size of the piece being hung, but the problem is most serious in the positioning of small objects.

Fig. 2-7. Nail a sawtooth hanger to an object's back at a point that provides for proper balance.

We avoid this difficulty by drilling a small hole on the back of the object so it can be hung directly on a nail. You must angle the hole into the back with a ³/₁₆-inch bit or slot it with a keyhole cutter in a drill. Either way, a slight lip will be produced at the top of the hole for catching the head of the nail. When making the hole, locate the point of suspension above center along the vertical "balance" line. A pointed awl is helpful in selecting a good spot (FIGS. 2-8 and 2-9). You should also align the piece with vertical and horizontal lines or edges of woodwork in the background.

Fig. 2-8. Use a pointed instrument on an irregular piece to determine a spot for drilling and hanging or for attaching a metal hanger.

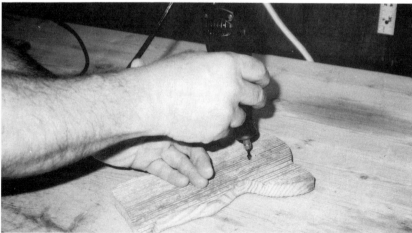

Fig. 2-9. Eliminate the need for a metal hanger by cutting a "keyslot" hole at the point of suspension.

LETTERING AND STENCILING

The walls, chairs, and lettered plaques in an authentically decorated country home are sometimes extensively ornamented by stenciling. All you need to stencil is a stencil (pattern) cut to the desired shape, a brush for the purpose, and thick paints.

You can buy stencils made of translucent plastic in many craft shops. The designs vary considerably, but most are generally appropriate for a country decor. Borders, alphabets, animals, and floral patterns in many sizes and shapes make up the usual selection (FIG. 2-10).

Fig. 2-10. The stenciling of walls along trim and corners of a room is indicative of an early means of decorating the country home.

If a suitable design is not available, you can make a design of your own with stiff paper, a plastic sheet, or cardboard. A sharp, pointed knife will allow you to cut sharp details (FIG. 2-11). Such stencils have practical limitations in time and the complexity of details, so it is seldom advisable to make complete alphabets of letters when so many ready-made varieties are available.

Stencils cut from thin plastic have several advantages. Besides their

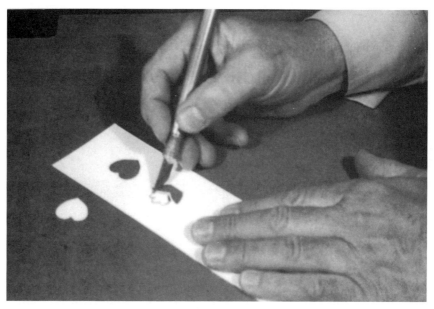

Fig. 2-11. Specially made templates can be used for stenciling or for tracing the outlines to guide the painting of repeated details.

transparency, which aids in maintaining alignment, they can be easily cleaned and used time and again. Other porous materials could absorb the paint and spread it over the wood where you don't want it.

You should observe some precautions when using stencils. First of all, the paint must be fairly dry and thick so it will not flow beyond the area where it is applied. Use a dabbing motion of the applicator, rather than brushing, to produce the proper result. Also, keep in mind that thin paints and inks disperse throughout the grain of some species of wood if they aren't first sealed with a transparent finish.

Secondly, make sure the spacing is visually pleasing by balancing areas among characters and words in lettered matter. A measured distance of equal linear dimension between all letters often produces an uneven appearance. Instead, draw light guidelines and roughly sketch in the complete wording to position the stencil. You can easily erase these guidelines when the paint has dried.

PAINTING AND STAINING

Wooden articles made in the country manner are almost invariably given a flat (non-glossy) finish. The implication of aging is one reason; the effect of hiding a sometimes evident roughness of surface is another. Acrylics, with their uniformity of coating and dullness when dry, provide an ideal solution.

The finishing of articles in a professional manner rests on the variety of acrylic paints at hand and the skill used in their application. Obviously the average person won't have a complete array of the colors and shades produced for this work. Black, white, and the primary colors (red, yellow, and blue) are the minimum necessary. Then, if you don't have a particular hue you can experimentally mix small quantities until you reach a suitable result.

As an alternative when coloring, or as a way of increasing the choices of colors available, you can use latex wall paints; however, use only the flat variety and thin it with water to improve the consistency for craftwork. The main disadvantage of latex paint is a slightly increased drying time.

You can also use wiping stains for finishing. They, too, dry to a uniform flatness. Oil-based stains are preferable because water-based stains tend to raise the grain of the wood, requiring moistening and additional sanding before staining.

Whether used alone or in combination, stains and paints should be protected with a sealer, although sealing is more important for some pieces than others. A coat or two of sealer from a spray can dries quickly and somewhat shields the finish from rubbing off. In addition, sealing keeps the surface from discoloring due to absorbing dust and oil—a matter of greatest importance for pieces subject to frequent or prolonged handling. A cardboard box with one side cut out helps to protect the surrounding environment when applying the spray to small articles (FIG. 2-12).

Fig. 2-12. Objects stained or painted in a flat finish should be sealed with a matte (non-glossy) material.

Always select your sealer according to the reasoning behind the paints you chose. In other words, use a matte sealer (for its non-glossy effect) over flat-finish paints. This recommendation holds whether you use a spray lacquer on "indoor" pieces, or a more durable, exterior grade of polyurethane for items to be placed outside in the lawn or garden.

Polyurethane—available in interior, exterior, and multi-purpose grades—makes an excellent finish for woods finished in the natural. Keep mineral spirits on hand to clean brushes used with polyurethane.

3

Colorful Cutouts

People who decorate their homes with country art frequently display figures made from flat boards. They hang the large pieces in clear view on the walls and stand the small ones on open shelves and mantels. The subjects preferred, as often as not, are rustic representations of the animals and people generally associated with life on the farm.

FORMING FLAT FIGURES

To make a cutout, select a flat board that has a 1-inch nominal thickness and few knots. Trace the figure's outline onto the board in a clear spot; then saw along the pencilled outline with a fine-bladed tool. Keep the cut smooth in order to avoid extensive sanding later. Use a scroll saw for this purpose, because its thin blade can be easily directed into sharp corners and will work handily when making internal cuts (FIG. 3-1).

Finish shaping the figure by sanding. If you have one, use a drum sander mounted in a drill press or hand drill for the initial sanding of a piece's edge (FIG. 3-2). Remove sharp corners and any surface roughness by hand sanding.

Complete each cutout by applying stain or acrylic paints (or both) and a sealer. Use the acrylics at full strength on the bare wood. Apply the whites first and add the decorative details last. Protect the finish from soiling by spraying on a coat of matte, transparent sealer made for the purpose.

Fig. 3-1. *A scroll saw is especially useful when sawing internal edges and sharp curves.*

Fig. 3-2. *Drum sanding quickly removes unwanted roughness along the profile of an irregular shape.*

Hung-Up Horse

Once it was domesticated to the bridle, the horse became a virtual necessity to man. How it eventually came to be so commonly copied in the design of toys is understandable due to the animal's tamed strength, gentle spirit, and familiarity as a model. Youngsters nearly everywhere have experienced, at one time or another, the joy of swaying back and forth on a copy built on rockers. From the rocking horse came hanging decorations of similar design, with many a mother finding the pieces excellent for the nursery.

A hanging horse of the kind shown in FIG. 3-3 might appeal to children, so it should be cute. A stylized, almost human, shaping of the eye helps to achieve the desired effect. Parental love can be signified by conventionalized arrangements of hearts.

Materials	*Tools*
1 × 10 board	scroll saw or jigsaw
acrylic paints	drill and 1/4″ bit
knitting yarn (for the mane)	sanding block and abrasive
quick-setting household	paper
cement	artist's brushes

Fig. 3-3. A hanging decoration makes an effective addition to the nursery.

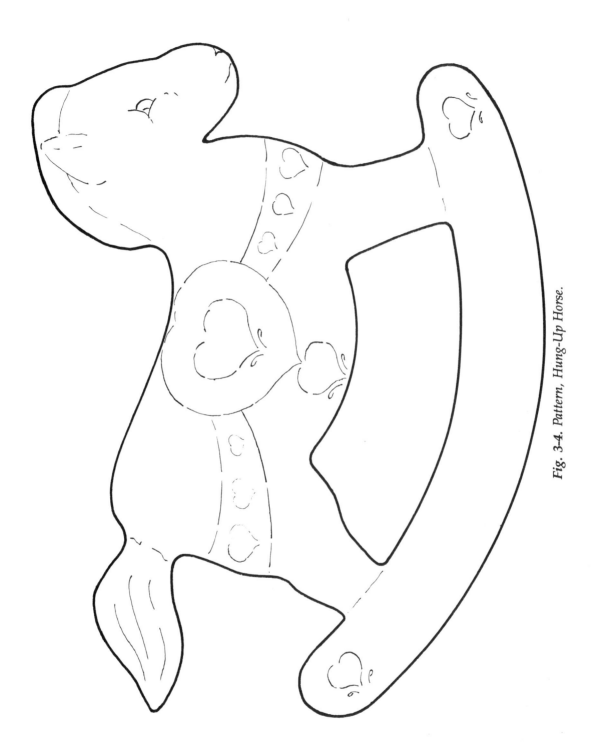

Fig. 3-4. Pattern, Hung-Up Horse.

After drawing the outline (see pattern, FIG. 3-4) and sawing the outside to shape, select a drill bit of diameter large enough to receive the saw blade. Drill a hole in the area between the legs, insert the saw blade, and saw completely about the internal profile. Sand all surfaces in the usual manner, and complete the construction by providing a means of hanging the piece.

Decorate the horse with acrylics of appropriate color. Paint the broad areas first and add the details last. If you use guidelines, sketch them in lightly so they can be covered by paint or be completely removed by erasing. Add names and dates if you like.

Close Couples and Solemn Singles

Of the many different domestic animals once commonly kept on the farm, few made more appealing subjects than the feathered creatures farmers allowed to roam about the barnyard. Perhaps a loyal dog or a cuddly cat were the prized ones of the lot, but ducks, geese, and chickens occupied a close second. Unlike the many animals that had to be fenced in, a farmer's fowl always seemed to come home to roost on their own, but then they were not housed on specialized farms as they are today. The familiar figures with their customary honking, quacking, clucking, and crowing are seldom seen or heard anymore by casual observers of rural Americana. Wooden simulations of the figures, as in FIG. 3-5, now generally serve in nostalgic remembrance.

Fig. 3-5. These country couples show several of the possible variations in size and style.

Larger animals customarily kept on the farm also may be given an expressiveness. The sheep (FIG. 3-6) exhibit an appearance of quiet and solemn contentment. You can change the expressions easily by altering the details about the eyes.

Materials

softwood board of 1″ nominal
    thickness
acrylic paints and sealer
narrow ribbon

Tools

scroll saw
sanding block with medium
    and fine abrasive paper
artist's brushes

Fig. 3-6. *The hearts represent a mutual fondness, while the eyes seem to reflect the warmth of a balmy afternoon.*

Refer to FIGS. 3-7 and 3-8 for the patterns. The method of producing simple cutouts follows the basic procedures for drawing a profile onto the wood, sawing around the outline, sanding the surfaces, and doing the decorating. We recommend using a scroll saw, but a hand-held jigsaw will also work. You could use a coping saw, but it is somewhat more difficult to control than power tools. A drill with sanding drums and abrasive sleeves is another alternative that will save time when smoothing roughly sawed edges.

When using the patterns for the animals, transfer only the outlines to the wood initially. Add the guidelines for details and limits for coloring (shown as fine marks on the drawings) after all sanding is done, if you add them at all. You can give some matched pairs identical shapes but different colors to distinguish the sexes. Add still more country flair by tying strips of calico ribbon around some of the figures.

Another common variation is to drill a hole into the top edge for holding a small candle. Always select a spot where the shape is appropriate for that application.

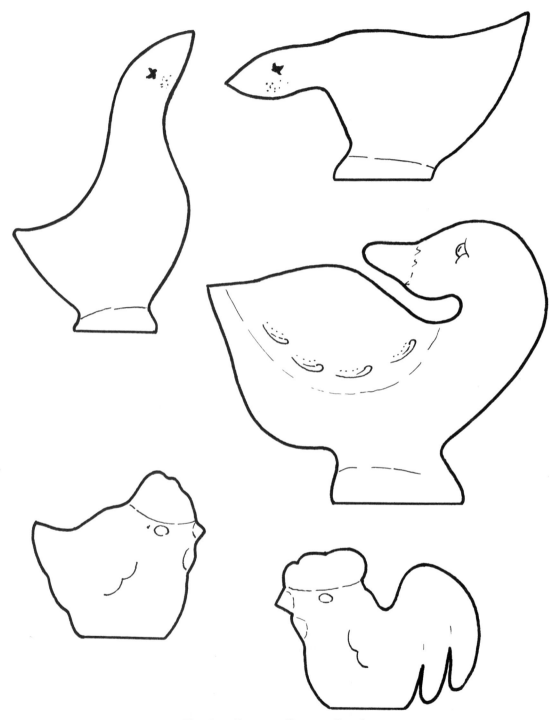

Fig. 3-7. Patterns, Country Couples.

Fig. 3-8. Patterns, Country Couples.

Basket Bearer

Another popular subject is the teddy bear, whether stuffed or made from wood. The cuddly appearance of the figure in one of its many variations makes an appropriate decoration or plaything. The general use of the figure in craftwork—a phenomenon probably never anticipated by Theodore "Teddy" Roosevelt when he saved a bear cub—seems to be evermore widespread.

A teddy bear made from a single piece of flat board is shown in FIG. 3-9. The effective use of stain and paint imparts a unique appearance to the wooden shape.

Materials
2 × 6 softwood, 10″ long
course, medium, and fine
  sandpaper
walnut stain and assorted
  acrylics
small basket (optional)

Tools
jigsaw or band saw
router and rounding bit or rasp
artist's brushes

Fig. 3-9. A teddy bear cut from a thick piece of wood can be a unique way to present candies in a small basket.

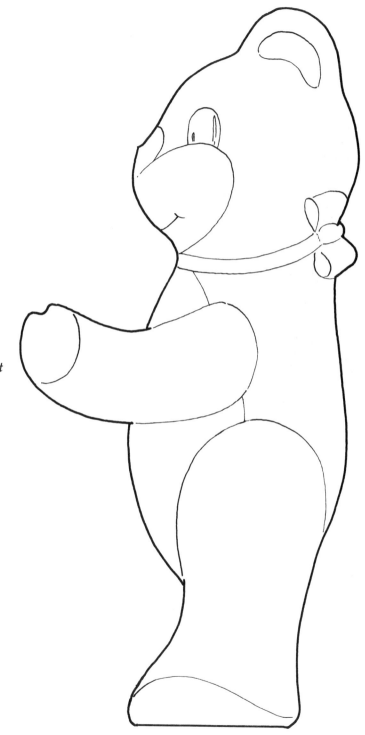

Fig. 3-10. Pattern, Basket Bearer.

This cute little fellow is made the same as other cutouts when shaped from flat stock, except for the rounding operation. The use of wood of $1^1/_2$-inch thickness makes possible the severe rounding of edges to impart somewhat of an appearance of depth, and it also enables the finished article to stand upright with reasonable stability.

Follow the usual order when making the bear, referring to the pattern, FIG. 3-10. Trace the figure's outline onto the wood, saw it to shape, round the edges on both sides, and prepare the figure for the finish coats by sanding (FIG. 3-11). Now wipe on the stain in the areas not to be otherwise colored.

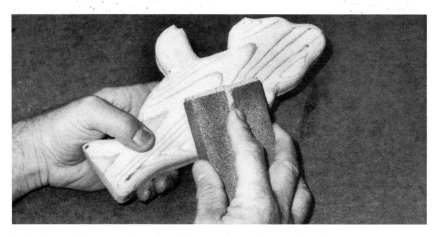

Fig. 3-11. Give the shaped wood a final sanding by hand to remove any tool marks.

When the stain has dried, paint the broad areas on both sides and edges. Add the details for the nose, eyes, and ears. As a final step in construction, carefully paint the thin black lines; these serve as boundaries while accenting the broader areas of color.

Rust and cream colors trimmed in black make an excellent combination on this piece. A light blue or green for the bow, when shaded with black to show folds, produces contrast and a sense of depth.

Consider ways to display your finished creation. One way is to fill the basket with small candies and suspend it from the bear's arms. Then place the little creation where your guests can see it. They will not always eat any of the sweets, but in all probability they will comment about the clever display.

Amish Couples

Probably no group is more readily identified with rural life and farming than the Amish. Their plain dress remains practically the same in style as it was several centuries ago, and it immediately signifies a traditional and austere manner of living.

Because of the customary quaintness and the clean life associated with them, images of the "plain folk" are now popular decorations about the home. A fireplace mantel makes a particularly good location for a pair of the cutouts. Figures 3-12 and 3-13 show couples made for standing. Patterns for these are provided in FIG. 3-14.

Materials	*Tools*
3/4" board of width to suit	scroll saw or jigsaw
acrylics and sealer	sanding block and abrasives
	artist's brushes

Fig. 3-12. *Just plain folk in their Sunday finest are familiar figures in some rural areas.*

Fig. 3-13. *The day of farmer's market is always a big occasion for the Amish.*

Fig. 3-14. Patterns, Amish Couples.

The choice of acrylics for Amish figures is the only thing substantially different from the basic procedures we explained. Amish customarily wear black garments, but with shirts and dresses often of plain, dark colors. Dark blue, green, and mauve are favorites. Red or any gaudy color would be too worldly and not in keeping with the lifestyle of the Amish, so choose and apply acrylics accordingly.

Human faces are customarily painted on wooden images with flesh-colored acrylics, although a flat white might be more effective on small figures. Facial details are never shaded and are often omitted entirely, suggesting a general lack of sophistication in both painting and subject.

4

Miniatures
and Magnets

Objects in miniature have always been prized in America. Even among the settlers it was common practice for the head of the household to spend free moments fashioning wooden figures in sizes greatly reduced from the originals. Some were copied from pieces developed in Europe, and others were created from memory or from real life. Among the common applications were simple imitations of animals and humans made for entertaining the youngsters. Noah's ark was especially popular. In fact, the set was one of the few playthings children in puritanical homes were permitted to have on Sunday.

Today, miniatures are as popular as ever. The small figures can be seen in use primarily as decorations on shelves, dresses, and kitchen appliances. Flat stock, sawed to the desired profile—with square rather than shaped edges—and features painted in flat colors are now commonplace. The subjects ordinarily show no particular emotion. More often they lack artistic refinement and display a quaintness of style, such as polka dots on a calico cat. The making of such miniatures can be as interesting as the displays themselves.

MINI MAKING

Although the shaping of an object to almost any smaller-than-actual scale is *miniaturization*, the term applies most often, as here, to extreme reductions in size. This extensive reduction of copies makes little difference in construction. You still cut them to shape with a scroll saw and brush acrylics onto the wood in the usual way. The standard practice of using 3/4-inch pine when making pieces for standing on edge also applies, regardless of scale. The only difference comes about when you prepare thinner pieces for clipping to a dress or for fastening to a refrigerator. In such cases, you would fill and sand plywood of 1/8- or 1/4- inch thickness carefully along the edges before painting. The use of hardboard might also change the procedure because a profile is easier to follow if you draw it on a piece primed in white (FIG. 4-1).

Fig. 4-1. *Hardboard painted in a flat white helps ease the sketching and sawing processes.*

ATTACHING MAGNETS, CLASPS, AND CORDS

The procedures for attaching magnets to wooden stick-ups and clasps to brooches are similar. Use either a strong, quick-setting household glue or epoxy (FIG. 4-2), and apply the suggested amount. To be certain of a good bond, test the strength of the joint when the adhesive has fully set.

For decorative pairs of objects fastened together with a cord, as for hanging from a Christmas tree, use a slightly different approach. First, drill holes at points of attachment, making them just large enough to receive the knotted ends of the cord. Apply adhesive to the cord's ends, force the tacky knots into the holes with a toothpick, and wipe away any excess glue. Paint or decorate the pieces as desired. You might consider using rub-on decorations, as in FIG. 4-3, as an acceptable alternative to painting small figures.

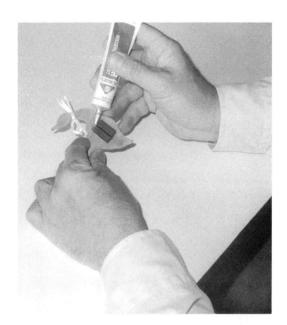

Fig. 4-2. A quick-setting household glue or epoxy is recommended for attaching magnets.

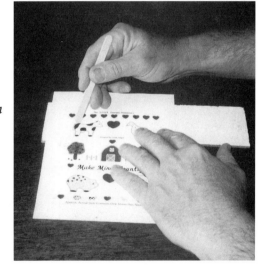

Fig. 4-3. Rub-on transfers, an alternative to paint, can be applied to the backing before sawing it to shape.

The materials necessary for attaching minis are available in various sizes. You can purchase thin magnetic strips of different widths at well-stocked craft or hobby shops, although you can sometimes salvage an ample quantity of a heavier variety from the door lining of a discarded refrigerator. You can purchase clasps in several lengths for making brooches and heavy cord for combining pairs at variety stores.

Fashionable Figures

Thin pieces in the form of garden vegetables for sticking to metal appliances, cuddly animals for attaching to garments, and decorative flowers paired for hanging from pegs or from Christmas tree branches are among the favorite applications. Separate pieces made from thick wood are suitable for standing on a shelf or in a shadow box. Examples of the variations are suggested by FIG. 4-4. The heart, here shown with a cord attached, is a shape that serves effectively in several applications.

Materials

3/4" pine for the standing
   miniatures
1/4" wood or hardboard for
   magnets and brooches
magnetic strips and brooch
   clasps
epoxy or contact glue
acrylic paints and sealer

Tools

scroll saw with a fine blade
sanding block with medium
   and fine abrasive papers
knife or scissors for sizing
   magnetic strips
artist's brushes for background
   and fine detailing

Fig. 4-4. Miniatures in a wide variety of shapes can be easily crafted from flat stock.

Fig. 4-5. Pattern, Fashionable Figures.

FLOUR

SUGAR

TEA

Use the patterns in FIG. 4-5 for making your minis. Sand small, thin cutouts with abrasive paper folded for easy control by hand. Usually, the only sanding necessary is to remove any roughness along edges and to smooth flat surfaces before sawing out the shapes.

Fig. 4-6. One of the many possible designs of a decorative candleholder.

Whatever your purpose in making miniscule decorations in wood, the procedures for their shaping are basically the same as for all country pieces, large and small. The form of attachment sometimes makes a difference because any hanging pieces will need to be drilled about 1/4-inch deep to receive the knotted ends of the cord.

The painting of fine details is generally left as the last operation. When you are deciding about finish, keep in mind that you can achieve striking results with little effort—one-color figures, small patterns, and light detailing can produce effective results.

Delightful Decorations

Colorful candleholders and corded cutouts make interesting decorations. Small figures of animals drilled for holding rattail candles are excellent adornments for a knickknack shelf in a country home (FIG. 4-6). Miniature cutouts with a heavy cord attached make beautiful decorations for the Christmas tree, especially if you give them traditional holiday shapes.

Cord

Candle

Fig. 4-7. Pattern, Delightful Decorations.

Materials

3/4" softwood for the candleholders

3/4" or thinner wood or
  hardboard for hanging pieces

sandpaper

heavy cotton cord

household cement

ribbon (optional)

rattail candles

acrylics, stain, and sealer

Tools

scroll saw

drill and bits

brushes

Select a pattern from FIG. 4-7 or adapt your own for the cutout, and sand in the usual way. Drill holes for the candles and cord before painting. Select drill diameters according to the sizes of the pieces to be inserted; usually diameters of 1/4 inch and 1/8 inch are adequate. Make the holes for the rattail candles about 1/2 inch deep and those for the knotted ends of the cord approximately 1/4 inch deep. When making corded miniatures, drill holes in the tops of pairs to make hanging easy when the ends of a 10-inch cord are glued in place.

Fig. 4-8. Bunnies and bears are favorite figures in country art.

Proceed with finishing in the manner explained for larger flat pieces. When you are deciding on the finish, bear in mind that not all items need a naturalistic appearance. You can impart a unique, simplified appearance by staining or painting an article entirely in a single color.

Bears, Bunnies, and Buildings

Both adults and children like things of reduced size. Youngsters prefer those made for play, while people of more advanced years tend to use the pieces for decorative purposes. That difference can be important in construction. Items to be used by very small children should be made solid, smooth, and somewhat larger than true miniatures. Greater leeway in construction may be realized when making items for older, more careful children and adults. The examples presented in FIGS. 4-8 and 4-9 are essentially decorative. Their use in play should be permitted only with proper instruction or supervision.

Fig. 4-9. Examples of the extensive number of different representations of buildings in greatly reduced size.

Materials

$^3/_4$" pine or other softwood
$^1/_8$" and $^1/_4$" plywood or
  hardboard
magnetic strips, brooch pins,
  and cord
epoxy or contact cement
stain, acrylic paints, and sealer

Tools

scroll saw with a fine blade
sanding block and abrasive
  papers
trimming scissors or knife
artist's brushes and wiping
  cloth

After tracing a pattern (FIGS. 4-10 and 4-11) saw the piece to shape, sand lightly, and brush on the background acrylic. Next, provide the miniature with a fastener (if desired) and paint the details. Don't overlook the advantage of making a number of cutouts to paint all at once. A walnut stain is an effective way to color some pieces before adding the final details.

Fig. 4-10. Patterns, Bears and Bunnies.

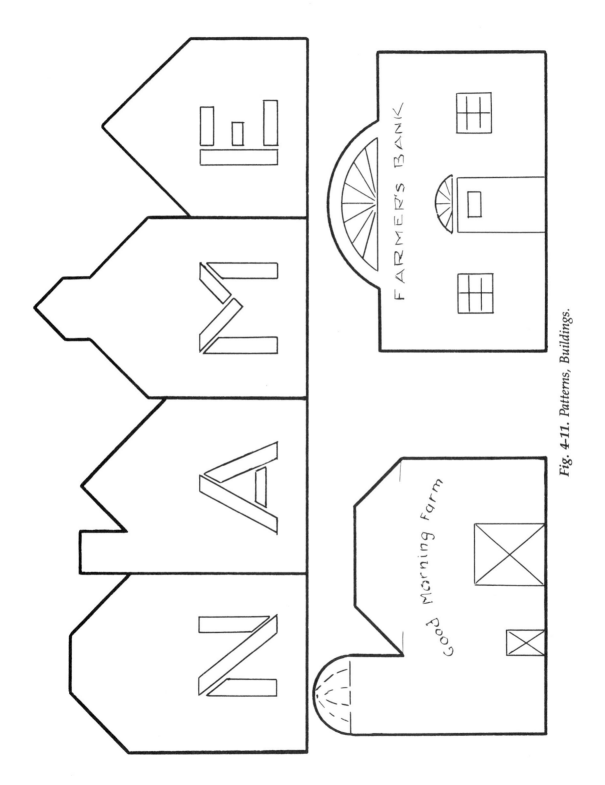

Fig. 4-11. Patterns, Buildings.

5

Attractive Assemblies

Country figures are frequently assembled from two or more pieces of wood because of appearance, although the requirements of construction sometimes take precedence. Pieces are added to the body of a cutout to form projecting ears and limbs or simply to make a base for supporting bulky figures in an upright position. As a result of this method, depth of form generally becomes more noticeable.

SHAPING AND ASSEMBLING

In the process of construction, built-up shapes often require more tools and thicker wood than normally needed for flat figures. The use of spruce or pine wood of 2-inch nominal thickness, while good for showing depth, requires sawing with a tool of greater capacity than that of an ordinary scroll saw. A band saw is particularly useful, but a less expensive, hand-held jigsaw will usually do. Always remove the sharp edges of thick pieces either by routing or by rasping and sanding. Edges that are sufficiently rounded give the figures a realistic appearance. Several operations are shown in FIGS. 5-1 and 5-2.

When you attach parts of assemblies, use a practical means, such as a quick-setting woodworker's glue. With such a glue, you'll only need to clamp laminations for about 30 minutes. A drill, bits, and wood screws or dowels are essential for securing pieces to end grain (FIG. 5-3).

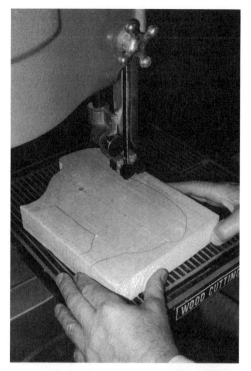

Fig. 5-1. Thick stock can often be most easily cut to form on a bandsaw.

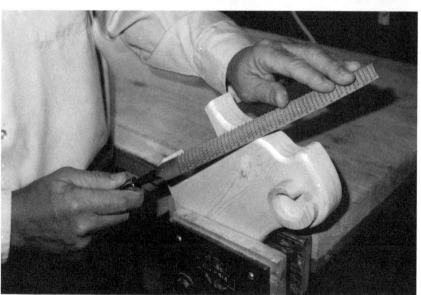

Fig. 5-2. The appearance of objects of $1^1/_2$ inch or greater in thickness is improved by rounding the edges.

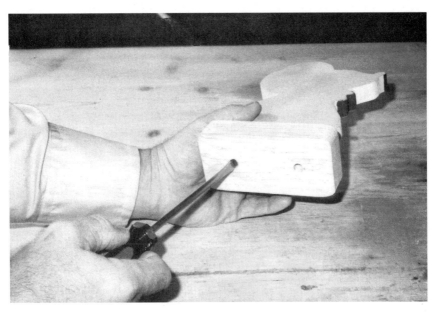

Fig. 5-3. *Wood screws or glued dowels will hold a base securely to an object's end grain.*

You should also consider using materials other than wood and paint for your assembled pieces. Miniature straw hats, small reed baskets, artificial flowers, and decorated cloth ribbons often add interest to country creations. Their effective use imparts the distinctive element of cuteness or quaintness that has become characteristic of country creations. Cleverness aside, some materials are useful solely for their realistic effect. Examples are: broom straw for a hen's nest, heavy cord to represent a mouse's tail, unraveled twine arranged to simulate the mane of a horse, and pumpkin seeds placed in the manner of flower petals. The possibilities seem endless. An inactive imagination is the only real deterrent to developing other applications.

Ordinarily, you should glue on material used for special effects. Sometimes, drilled sockets are necessary, but try gluing before making holes. We recommend a quick-setting household glue—one that sets up in five minutes or less. Such glue is practically indispensable because you can't always clamp easily or for extended periods of time.

Colorful Weathercock

A representation of a sunrise signaler makes an attractive display above the fireplace mantel of a home decorated in the country manner. The design of the piece in FIG. 5-4, a simulated weathercock, is an adaptation from Early American forms that were attached to arrows and made for rotating above roof peaks. Original designs of the rooster were used for symbolic purposes on church buildings. Their general use as indicators of wind direction came later.

Materials
rooster—1 × 8 pine board, 9″ long
arrow—2 3/4″ dia. ×
    17 1/2″ pine strip
dowel—3/8″ dia. × 1 3/4″
woodworker's glue
acrylic paints of various colors

Tools
scroll saw or jigsaw
drill with 1/4″ and 3/8″ bits
sanding block and abrasive
    paper
artist's brushes
artist's brushes

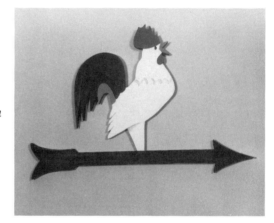

Fig. 5-4. A rooster on a weather arrow represents a tradition of long standing in rural America.

As you can see from the materials list and the pattern (FIG. 5-5), the weathercock can be made from a softwood board in two pieces. The pieces are held together with a dowel and glue. You can eliminate the doweling and gluing operation by cutting the weathercock in one piece from a sheet of plywood. To do that, first align the pattern for tracing so that the foot of the rooster is centered end-to-end on the arrow.

To assemble separate pieces, drill through the arrow's shaft at mid-point and into the foot of the rooster to a depth of 1 inch for the dowel. You can get perfect alignment by clamping the arrow and the rooster's foot together so you can drill a hole through the shaft into the leg in one operation. Glue the dowel in place with the exposed end flush with the bottom surface of the shaft.

Prepare the piece for hanging by angling a drill-point into the back-side at the balance point. Finish the front of the assembly with acrylics of appropriate colors. Try for an additional touch of authenticity by giving the painted edges a final sanding to imitate aging.

Dowel O.C.

Fig. 5-5. Pattern, Colorful Weathercock.

Duck by Candlelight

As shown in FIG. 5-6, a beautifully shaped duck, accented with a ribbon and an open heart, stands attached to a base to which a candle cup has been fastened. A glass holder rests on the wooden cup, thereby, permitting safe burning of the short candle. The piece makes an exceptional decoration, especially when paired with a similar figure of reverse form.

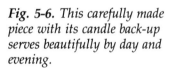

Materials

duck—1 × 8 board, 7″ long
base—4¹/₂″ × 5¹/₂″ section of
  board
dowels (2)—¹/₄″ dia. × 1″
woodworker's glue
acrylic paints and sealer
silk ribbon, ¹/₄″ wide

Tools

scroll saw or jigsaw
drill with ¹/₄″ bit
wood clamp
sanding block and abrasive
  papers
artist's brushes

Fig. 5-6. This carefully made piece with its candle back-up serves beautifully by day and evening.

Pattern tracing, scroll sawing, and finishing with acrylics follow procedures previously given for making flat board cutouts. (Use FIG. 5-7 for the pattern.) In this project, however, you must join the base firmly to the upright piece. Glue alone might do, but doweling makes a stronger, more secure joint. Doweling through the front is acceptable, providing the inserts are perfectly flush with the face of the assembly. Cover any

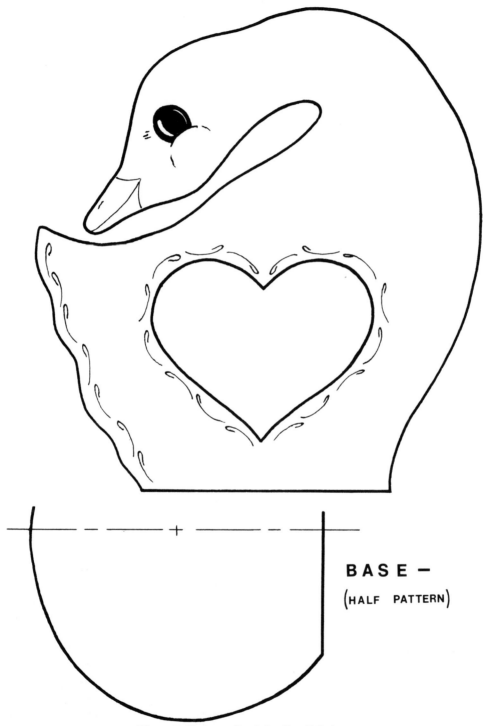

BASE –
(HALF PATTERN)

Fig. 5-7. Pattern, Duck by Candlelight.

chipping around the holes or unevenness at the dowels' ends with wood filler, and sand the surfaces flush so that no unevenness shows through the acrylic finish.

The choice of acrylics for the project depends somewhat on personal preference. An off-white for the body and yellow-orange for the bill make good selections. Edge-trimming done in champagne or light blue adds a bit of elegance, but any number of different colors would do equally well for the trim. In any case, use a ribbon of matching color for a unifying effect.

Big-Eared Bunnies

Another effective way to make country creations is to use thick wood entirely and let the grain show. The sparse use of acrylics adds to a piece's effectiveness. Because the treatment of facial features can make a big difference in such applications, try to create the less aggressive, tender expressions people would prefer to see in their homes. Figure 5-8 displays a somewhat timid expression.

Materials
center piece—
 $1^1/2'' \times 5'' \times 9''$ pine
appendages (2)—
 $1^1/2'' \times 6'' \times 9''$ overall
woodworker's glue
1″ brads and plastic wood
black, white, and rust acrylics
 and sealer
rust-colored ribbon with small
 pattern

Tools
band saw or jigsaw
flat chisel, nail set, and
 hammer
router with $^3/8''$-radius
 rounding bit or a rasp
sanding device with abrasives
hand clamp and bench vise
detail brushes

Fig. 5-8. Simplicity of design and construction result in a modern piece of country art.

You'll need to observe several special procedures in making this rabbit. Make all of the appendages 1½ inches thick, except for the front legs, which can be made more realistic by first planing the wood to about one-inch thickness. Saw out the parts with the grain lengthwise, and round the edges with a router or rasp. (Rasping, whether done by hand or a rotary power-tool, requires the most sanding.) Use a chisel to taper the ears, and pare them flat as shown in the section of the pattern drawing (FIG. 5-9).

Additionally, observe that the pattern for one ear has been turned upward, even though it, too, is a duplicated profile. When attaching the pieces, hold the ears in place with sunken brads and glue. You can clamp other parts easily while the glue is setting.

For those who consider the shaping of the ears to be a problem, we've suggested an alternate arrangement in a second pattern (FIG. 5-10). In this design, leave the sawed pieces with square edges, and make the pairs of ears and legs from thinner material than that used for the body.

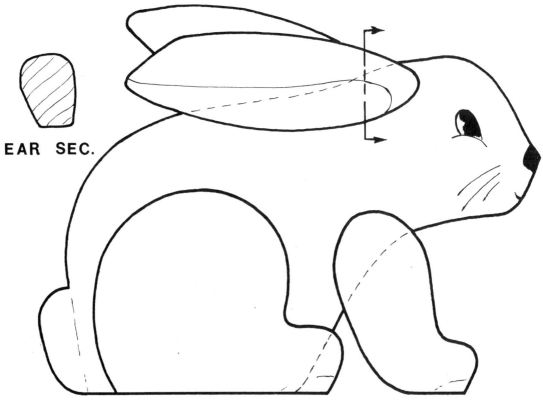

EAR SEC.

Fig. 5-9. Pattern, Big-Eared Bunny.

This Amish couple and their farm animals are examples of country cutouts that will add charm to any home decor.

This delightful weathercock can serve its original purpose outdoors, or it can be paired with other country creations for a unique look.

Paints and brushes are ready to bring your projects to life.

Painting the finishing touches on the mouse's eye.

Cute and humorous country creations, like this mouse, are sure to bring smiles to the younger set.

Power tools, such as the drill and jigsaw, make detailed tasks a breeze.

Hand-sanding using a wood block is the best way to round the edges of your wooden project.

This bear offers candies from his little basket.

This little step stool is perfect in any home decor . . .

And it doubles as a child's seat, too!

This sulking chair, with its hand-painted details, makes a wonderful gift.

This pretty candle holder will soften a room with candlelight.

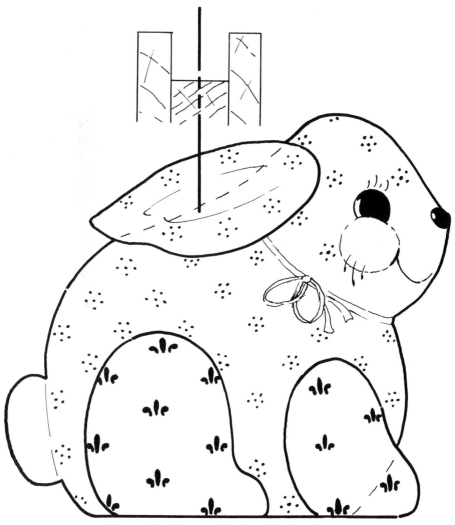

Fig. 5-10. Alternate Design, Big-Eared Bunny.

Such differences in thickness give the figure a realistic appearance, even though the edges remain relatively sharp.

You can alter the amount of painting you do to suit your taste. The patterns themselves are country in character, so use your imagination.

6

Mottos and Messages

Signs with "homey" greetings are becoming familiar sights today. Wooden plaques that contain wording of a country flavor are often hung for the benefit of a home's occupants as much as for the visitors.

The style of letters chosen depends, aside from personal preference, on ease of application and reading. Whether it is done entirely freehand, entirely with a stencil, or partly with both (a stencil outline filled in freehand), lettering can convey the impression of a loving, caring household. A simple "welcome" is a common greeting near the main entrance of a home (FIG. 6-1), but another location is reserved for such statements as "back door friends are best." Pious statements seeking blessing for the home are also common in this form of decoration.

Holiday greetings are another practical application. Figure 6-2 suggests how effective a country creation can be when made for hanging at the appropriate time of year.

References to the family, to friends and friendship, and to love are especially popular. The wording often takes the form of a familiar slogan.

SAMPLE SLOGANS

About the home:

- Home Sweet Home
- There's no place like home. —J.H. Payne
- Home is where the heart is.
- Caring and sharing make a house a home.

Fig. 6-1. Both the message and the border on this plaque have been stenciled in place.

Fig. 6-2. Lettered creations effectively bring out the holiday spirit in a country setting.

Friends and friendship:

- Happiness is having friends.
- When a friend asks, there is no tomorrow. —Old Proverb
- Friendship is the elixir of life.

Love:

- Love is the marrow of friendship. —J. Howell
- Perfect love casteth out fear. —I John 4:18

Other catchphrases:

- Laughter is contagious.
- Count your blessings.
- Hospitality is homemade.

FORMS

You can make a wall plaque for a motto or message in the form of a farm animal or in a simple rectangular or oval shape with decorative border or partial edge design (FIG. 6-3).

Fig. 6-3. *Pattern, border and corner designs for freehand applications.*

Much of the lettering is done with stencils. You can make lettering stencils by hand in a chosen style, but a large variety of ready-made styles are available in craft stores. These commercially manufactured plastic pieces are convenient and suitable for ordinary purposes.

LETTERING BY STENCILING

A stencil for lettering is a thin sheet of plastic, hardboard, or other impervious material that has perforations in the style of an alphabet. Paint applied to one side of the sheet passes through the openings to form the characters on the surface against which the sheet rests. As long as you position the stencil properly, you can create letters, words, and phrases.

We recommend using stencils for the lettering on country signs because of their availability in various forms and their comparative ease in use, which allows you to avoid the more difficult task of shaping letters freehand. Be sure, though, that the alphabet you choose is legible and appropriate in size. Also, you must carefully plan the spacing between letters and words *visually* not mechanically.

When stenciling, use a brush with stiff bristles suitable for stippling. Hold it as shown in FIG. 6-4. Dab the paint (don't smear it!) using a thick mixture to avoid running or seeping into and spreading widely throughout the bare wood. Press the stencil firmly against its backing, and be sure the paint is dry before sliding the next character into position.

Fig. 6-4. The stenciling of letters requires skill in spacing and in painting.

You can clean up wet smears of acrylic paint with a wet paper towel. You can correct slight overruns most easily when the paint is dry, either by careful scraping or by covering them with the background color. Usually, the lettering is done after the background has been given the desired finish.

A Country Welcome

An effective, yet easily made, greeting sign is presented in FIG. 6-5. The figure is simple in shape, and the painting is flat and unshaded. Both the decorative heart and the lettering have been stencilled. The posture of the animal and the carefully detailed eye make the duck appear alert to visitors. Of course, any reluctance one might have on first seeing that expression would be quickly overcome by the warm greeting and the friendly symbol below.

Materials
$3/4'' \times 6^{1}/2'' \times 9''$ board or
$^{1}/2''$ plywood
assorted acrylics

Tools
scroll saw
sanding device with abrasives
drill and bits
artist's brushes
stencil and stencil brush

Fig. 6-5. A plaque with a simple greeting often fits nicely in a country decor.

Fig. 6-6. Pattern, Country Welcome.

Refer to FIG. 6-6 for the pattern. After sawing and sanding, locate the balance point of the piece and drill a slot into its back for hanging. You could attach a metal hanger instead, but then the piece would never fit entirely flush against the wall. In any case, remember to locate the point of suspension above the center of mass.

Paint the duck a flat white or off-white, the beak and feet yellow-orange, and the heart and tip of the tail a complementary color such as pale blue. Do the eye and letters in black so they stand out vividly.

Heartfelt Hello

Like the Gothic letters used in the previous project, the Roman forms also come in pre-cut stencils of various sizes. They are about as legible as the others but add a bit of variety due to the projecting serifs. Figure 6-7 shows an application in a prominent display.

Fig. 6-7. A dove-and-heart plaque suggests a particularly warm greeting for visitors.

This arrangement has considerable appeal for those who want to project the meaning symbolized by the heart between these two peaceable creatures. Historically, illustration often included instead a two-headed eagle with a breast drawn in the shape of a heart. Once a mark of the Roman Empire, the double eagle was commonly displayed in early America until its use on signs of taverns became commonplace. Consequently, references to the "split crow" disparaged the symbol and contributed to its disuse. A more positive symbol came to be preferred, with the heart and doves now almost totally replacing the sterner, more ferocious symbol of earlier times.

Materials	*Tools*
greeting strip—	scroll saw
$3/4'' \times 2^1/4'' \times 9^1/4''$	sanding device and abrasives
heart and doves—	drill and bits
$3/4'' \times 4^1/4'' \times 16''$	brushes
acrylic paints and spray sealer	
4 screw eyes ($1/2''$)	

Cut the pieces to size using FIG. 6-8 as a pattern. Round the edges, and fix the horizontal strip in place before slotting the back of the heart at the balance point. Drill pilot holes to ease the insertion of screw eyes.

Paint the doves colonial gray, feathering the edges lightly with an off-white. Use either thinned acrylic or wipe away some of the wet acrylic when feathering. Brush a deep red on the heart and letters for its effect as a complement to the gray. Seal the natural wood before stenciling the lettering and, as a final step, apply a decorative edging with the tip of a brush dipped in paint of contrasting color.

Rowdy Roosters

How a message is presented often determines its effectiveness. A bit of humor, an illustration of animals displaying a familiar attitude—especially one that represents a human characteristic—and wording that piques the imagination are among the possibilities for producing memorable displays. Belligerence could be represented by head-butting rams, obesity by an overstuffed pig, fright by a hair-ruffled cat, and contentment by a placidly smiling cow. You can represent almost any human trait with an animal, and when you add an impressive statement, the message will be complete and clearly conveyed.

The once-familiar scene of a pair of roosters fighting presents this kind of opportunity. Figure 6-9 shows an application. While the feathered shapes represent one thing, their squabbling and the lettered caption suggest another. The battling roosters might overlook a wiggly meal, but a comparable contention between two people leaves no room for acknowledging the positive accomplishments of either one. The subtlety of the presentation, then, softens the impact of the underlying point.

Fig. 6-8. Pattern, Heartfelt Hello.

Fig. 6-9. This once-common confrontation carries an important message for everybody.

Materials
3/4" × 9" × 20" pine board
3/4' × 2" × 20" pine strip
6 brass screw eyes
18" brass chain or wire
dark acrylic paint
polyurethane and mineral
   spirits

Tools
circular saw
hand plane or jointer
pliers
sanding block and fine
   abrasives
drill and bits
brushes

Select a board that has little likelihood of warping or cupping. Saw the pieces to size, plane the edges, and sand the surfaces with a fine grit. Finish the preparations by drilling pilot holes for the screw eyes.

Apply a thick acrylic (preferably a dark color for contrast) to the design, border, and letters. Although sealing the surface with a penetrating coat of polyurethane isn't entirely necessary, it does permit you to easily correct any errors you might make when painting.

Next, lightly pencil on or transfer the figures and letters using FIG. 6-10 as a pattern. Be careful to press lightly when making guidelines so

Fig. 6-10. Pattern, Rowdy Roosters.

you can erase them later. After painting, remove unwanted lines and brush on a final coat of polyurethane in readiness for the hardware.

While a block form of lettering is simple to do, you might want to use a completely different variety. Feel free to use a different caption, too, or a different border. (Perhaps you could choose an appropriate design from the examples given in FIG. 6-3.)

7

Comical Creations

While some creations are highly serious, others have a whimsical side. A bit of humor, whether accompanied by a thought-provoking message or not, can go a long way toward providing the moments of joy everyone needs. In this chapter, we provide a few tips on how to style figures whimsically or humorously to help the beginner create a comical country piece.

CREATING COMICAL CHARACTERS

An effective way to begin is to choose a likeable subject and give it an unusual twist. Sketch a number of views on paper and select the best one for the project. Try to arrive at a solution that conveys a thought and induces the viewer to smile or react mirthfully. Some suggestions:

Caricature a Figure Distort one or more of its features. Facial exaggerations are especially useful in showing mood, but the eyes are among the most expressive parts of all. Figure 7-1 shows an example in the sketching stage.

Give a Farm Animal Human Characteristics Although a form of caricaturing, this method is one of the most effective ways to create a funny piece.

Create an Uncommon Friendship A mutual attraction between a rabbit and a dog has interesting possibilities.

Add a Caption A brief, lettered message can clarify, contradict, show irony, create *entendre*, or serve a generally supportive role.

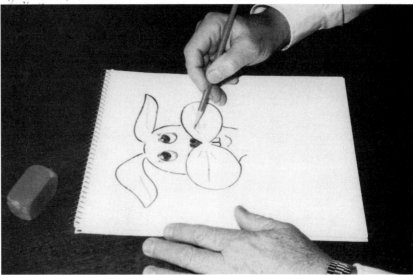

Fig. 7-1. Sketching is basic when working out a figure's expression and form.

Keep the Subject Positive Tragedy, ferocity, or any of a host of other negative emotions and feelings are generally inappropriate for country humor.

Two major problems confront the designer of a humorous piece: developing a workable idea or mental picture and putting it into a finished drawing. Undoubtedly, acceptable accomplishments in these areas are more likely to result from sincere effort and practice than innate talent. The person who devotes his attention to seeking humorous incidents will find that, ordinarily, family life and the daily workplace are replete with laughable occurrences. The concern then is to imagine how you can make one such situation into a suitable display in wood. You'll also want to think about how to give the idea a country flair.

The second point of concern, after you have developed a good idea, is to make a drawing of the idea so you can make it in the shop. Paper-and-pencil drawings are especially useful. They give you ample opportunity to make changes or develop entirely different designs and can even help you eliminate unwanted features before you begin constructing in wood.

The development of a plan for a cutout proceeds as presented in FIG. 7-2. The object in this case is to show a chicken struggling with *the early worm*. We chose a rooster for the illustration for its feathery form and distinctive identity. The caption on the wooden base gives the desired wrinkle, and the frazzled appearance of the bird supports the idea of weariness. Anyone who has had to arise at an early hour day after day can fully appreciate the implication of this message.

Outlining

Roughing-in

Finish Detailing

cord

dowel
to base

Why can't I sleep in just once?

Fig. 7-2. *Steps in preparing a drawing of humorous idea for a painted cutout.*

The first step in making a drawing of the rooster and worm requires a sheet of paper or cardboard large enough to accommodate the scene at the size you want. Then sketch lightly penciled ovals in the approximate positions and sizes in preparation for roughing-in locations of the details. Next, add the finished outline, details, and caption, and trace the finished profile onto wood or cut it into a template.

"You Do It"

Test your skill at creating humor. Begin by observing the assembly in FIG. 7-3 and try to develop a caption of your own. Following the applicable parts of the instructions, you might be surprised at the variety of possibilities you can develop on your own.

Fig. 7-3. A number of different captions could aptly express this pullet's consternation.

Start by concentrating on the subject. Here is a pullet who is, for some reason, unable to lay an egg in the usual form. The idea presented is this: If I don't do something the way you want it done, *then do it yourself!*

With this thought in mind, list on a sheet of paper all the possible comments you might consider. The more comments the better: Whether some are wild and unrealistic makes no difference, because the longer the list the more likely it is that several good captions will be created. Your caption could indicate a defensive or apologetic attitude, such as, "But I'm just a beginner," or "Some days nothing goes right." It might also make reference to sworn secrecy, a medical disability, a faulty operation, or the difficulty of the job. If your efforts result in more than one good caption, you might consider making several of the young hens for gifts.

Materials	*Tools*
body—3/4" × 5" × 8" overall	scroll saw
base—3/4" × 4¹/2" × 9"	sanding device
oval eggs (3)—	and abrasive paper
3/4" × 1" × 1¹/4"	drill and bits
square egg—3/4" × 1¹/4" sq.	screwdriver
cutout for caption—1/8"	artist's brushes
hardboard, approx. 2" × 3"	
1¹/4" FHB wood screw	
household cement	
acrylics and sealer	
stain and wiping cloth	

Figure 7-4 provides a pattern for the hen. The shaping of the hen and eggs follows the general steps for sawing and sanding other flat pieces, but you might find a drum sander in a drill press indispensable for the internal curves (FIG. 7-5). Similarly, a disk sander can be useful for smoothing flat surfaces and convex edges.

It is a good idea to do all painting and staining before assembling the parts. Set the finished eggs in spots of quick-drying household cement, arranging them so that the square one will be tilted toward the viewer. Add pieces of broken broom straw about the eggs to represent the nest. Fasten the hen and lettered piece to the base, and spray the complete assembly with a matte sealer.

Preferably, letter the caption freehand: The letters don't have to be precisely formed in this kind of application. A fine brush and black acrylic will do nicely. Lightly penciled guidelines will help keep the wording in line.

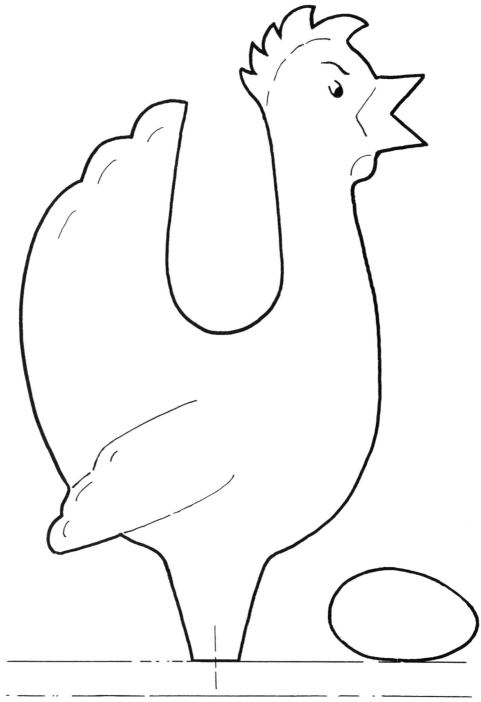

Fig. 7-4. Pattern, You Do It.

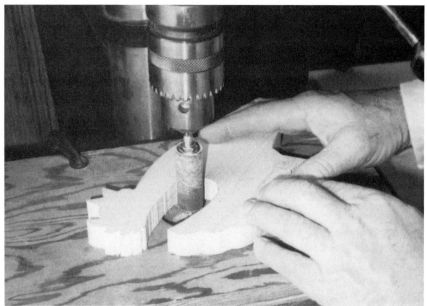

Fig. 7-5. A drum sander in a drill press is a practical way to smooth concavely curved surfaces.

Munching Mouse

Most mothers will quickly grasp the humor of the "munching mouse" in FIG. 7-6. What young son or daughter hasn't snitched a cookie or two at one time or another? Because the experience is so common, the cute little muncher makes a desirable addition beside a cookie jar in just about any kitchen.

Fig. 7-6. This cutie seems to have some difficulty hiding the goods.

WHAT COOKIE ?

Fig. 7-7. Pattern, Munching Mouse.

Materials
mouse—$3/4'' \times 6'' \times 7^{1}/4''$
base—$1^{1}/8'' \times 3'' \times 5^{1}/4''$
wood screws (2)—$1^{1}/2''$ FHB
acrylics and matte sealer

Tools
circular saw
scroll saw
sanding device
    and abrasive paper
drill and bits
artist's brushes

Refer to the pattern (FIG. 7-7) for tracing. Power saws of several varieties are practical tools for building country creations. A circular saw is especially useful for cutting the base, as the thick stock must be cut to length and beveled (FIG. 7-8). You can use either a scroll saw or jigsaw for the irregular contours.

Fig. 7-8. *A power saw simplifies the squaring and beveling of the base pieces.*

    After forming the mouse and its base, drill and counterbore for assembling the pieces. Paint the mouse before firmly fixing it in place. Use slightly thinned acrylics over background areas where a shaded effect is desired. Also, spray a light coating of sealer over the raw wood before applying the acrylics. Do that, too, for the piece to be lettered. The sealer will help keep the water-based paints from spreading throughout the wood's pores and raising the grain. Apply the sealer to the finished piece, as well.

Fat Cat

If you've ever seen an overweight cat drape itself lazily over a ledge or an arm of a sofa, you'll appreciate the built-up feline shown in FIG. 7-9. Besides being comical, it has the special quality of a country creation. Its dark body with seemingly worn edges, heart-shaped nose, calico-like legs, and simulated stitching about the face are indicative of the type.

The humor of this piece can be readily repeated by making a pair of kittens in similar reclining posture and finish (see pattern, FIG. 7-10). They might be called "Copy Cats."

Materials	*Tools*
3/4" pine for the body, legs, and back piece (the tail and right foot)	scroll saw
	sanding device and abrasives
	wood clamps
1/4" thickness of pine, plywood or hardboard for the face	artist's brushes
woodworker's glue	
acrylics and sealer	

Fig. 7-9. *Fat cats sometimes assume downright peculiar positions when sleeping.*

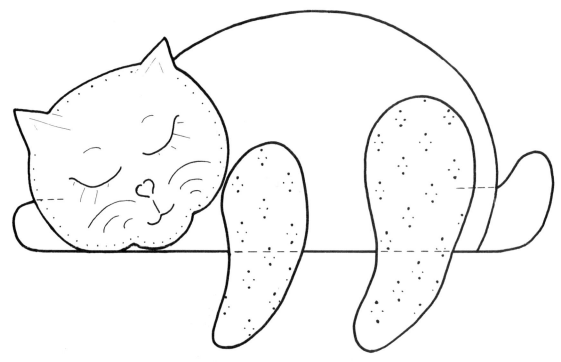

Fig. 7-10. Pattern, Fat Cat.

When cutting out the back piece, be aware that it extends fully from the tip of the tail to the tip of the foot. So made, it adds another 3/4 inch of bearing surface to the body. The combined 1¹/₂-inch thickness will rest securely on a shelf's edge.

The treatment around the face is another procedure that requires explanation. The body at that end follows the outline of the face piece. Saw the face piece to shape and glue it in place before attaching the back piece to the body. That way you can sand the outer edge of the face and body as a unit.

For variety, paint a different face on the cat. One alternative is to change the expression to a state of partial awakening.

Homey Humor

Cats and dogs are sometimes very chummy, but not often will a pair of them have an ecstatic moment like the one represented in FIG. 7-11. The facial expressions—though fictitious, indeed—emphasize the somewhat humorous relationship without appearing to be entirely unbelievable.

The lettered motto and hearts further support the concept. One would expect a warm atmosphere in a home that causes even unlikely affection to blossom.

Fig. 7-11. *As this couple shows, there's nothing quite like living in a peaceful and loving home.*

Materials	Tools
1 × 8 board for the couple	scroll saw
1 × 6 board for the motto	drill bits
2 dowel pins ³/₈″ dia. × 1¹/₂″	sanding device and abrasives
woodworker's glue	bar clamps
acrylic paints	artist's brushes
	lettering stencil

Fig. 7-12. Pattern, Homey Humor.

Fig. 7-13. Pattern, Homey Humor.

See the patterns in FIGS. 7-12 and 7-13. The two parts must be dowelled together at the proper point of alignment when cut from separate boards, but you can avoid that operation by sawing the assembly as a unit from a piece of plywood. Keep in mind that the use of plywood, as a rule, requires you to fill cavities and cover the laminates along the edges. However constructed, the unit is made ready for hanging in the usual manner.

When preparing to finish the article, select combinations of colors that generally harmonize yet provide enough contrast for the wording to be easily read. Also, keep the number of different colors to a minimum so you don't destroy the effect of unity. Plan to do the stencilling last, and remember to keep the *areas* between letters of a word about equal.

8

Household Holders

Some articles are made to be used not just as decorative pieces. Their main purpose is to make certain operations easier. Any decoration applied to such a form might enhance its appearance but, as was often the case in early times, the practicality of a piece remains the main concern.

Early rural settlers in this country had to provide for themselves most of the things they needed for day-to-day living. As often as not, they had to rely on limited knowledge and simple tools when fashioning the materials at hand into items of practical value. Their houses were built and warmed with timber cleared from the land in order to raise crops and vegetables, and the furniture and utensils often were shaped from hand-hewn slabs. Those initial creations were usually plain and sometimes even crude.

As time went by, people began to take greater pains to create wooden ware that was visually appealing. The use of color became more prevalent, with stenciling and hand-painting eventually gaining respectability as a means of decorating "fancy" things. Nonetheless, an object's use remained the basis for its form.

FASHIONING FUNCTIONAL FORMS

Any object intended for practical use must be made with a particular purpose in mind. Size, shape, and strength are basic considerations, but most other concerns are secondary. No matter how clever or lovely a piece might be, its value is limited if it does not work as it was intended.

Consider the design of a paper-napkin holder. Its basic requirement is to hold a quantity of napkins so that they can be seen and removed easily. In order to satisfy those needs, the napkins would be most presentable if they stood on edge in the open rather than in a pile in a lidded box. Two vertical pieces of wood held about 3 inches apart by a solid base serves effectively (FIG. 8-1), and the weight of the wood helps prevent upsetting. For the most functionality, the shape and size of the uprights must be made so that the upper edges of the napkins are in view. If the uprights are too large, it will be hard to grasp the napkins and remove them. If they are too small, the napkins will bend over.

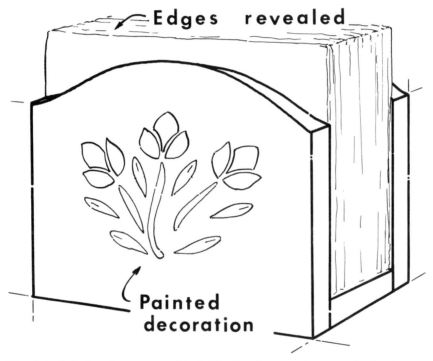

Fig. 8-1. *A design of a paper-napkin holder based on requirements for displaying and dispensing.*

You must also consider the function of the holder in finishing and decorating it. The surface must be smooth and impart no oil or color to the napkins. For that reason, you should give a stained holder a coat of clear sealer.

While many forms of decoration are not essential to an article's use, they do serve an important purpose. A painted design can improve appearance and impart a unifying decor. Decorating in the country manner, as in any other style, requires harmony of application for best effect.

Even more importantly, the shape of a painted design should complement the piece it decorates. Avoid the square-within-a-circle effect. Make your border designs follow the outlines of surfaces to be decorated, and relate each centrally placed figure to the project's profile. An example of a successful design application is presented in FIG. 8-2.

Fig. 8-2. A properly designed holder will adequately display either square or oblong napkins.

Applications like this one are sometimes best carried out by making a template (FIG. 8-3). A piece of thin cardboard works well, because the design can be readily cut out with a sharp knife. A section of a cereal box makes a rigid template that will hold up reasonably well under repeated use.

Fig. 8-3. A stencil cut from cardboard is especially useful in maintaining a symmetrical repetition of parts.

When possible, always give an article of high quality an extra touch to help make it exceptional. For example, place felt pads on the bottom corners of the napkin holder (FIG. 8-4). While this is not essential to the article's use, the pads have a cushioning effect that a frequent user of the item will appreciate.

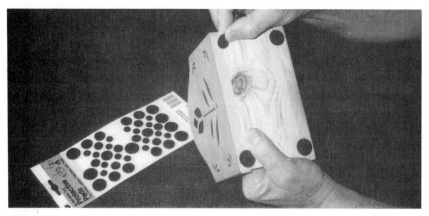

Fig. 8-4. *Self-sticking felt pads provide an extra measure of protection when positioning the holder.*

Decorative Towel Dispenser

You can make a unique, functionally designed accessory for the kitchen from dowel rods and two flat pieces of wood. The sawed-out heart capping the dispenser facilitates grasping when unrolling a towel (FIG. 8-5). The decorative heart also contains a doweled projection so that the user can remove the cap when changing paper rolls. Unlike commercially-made plastic holders, which must be fixed in place, this one can be moved around as needed. The assembly takes up only about 6 inches of space horizontally, but the attractiveness of the country motif is reason enough for keeping the holder in full view on the kitchen counter.

Materials

1" dia. × 12" dowel for the
  center rod
3/8" dia. × 1 1/4" dowel for the
  friction pin
3/4" × 4" sq. softwood for the
  heart
3/4" × 5 1/2" dia. piece for the
  base
woodworker's glue
acrylics and sealer

Tools

scroll saw
sanding device and abrasive
  paper
drill, twist bits, and 1"
wood-boring bit
artist's brushes

Fig. 8-5. *This easily made dispenser is both practical and decorative.*

As with most projects made from wood, there are several workable procedures for completing the steps (FIG. 8-6). For example, you can bore the holes to the required sizes with a brace and bit instead of with twist drills and wood-boring bit. Either way, the dowels should fit snugly and be perpendicular to the surfaces of the wood into which they are set and glued.

Moderately sand the part of the dowel friction pin that projects from the cap piece to ease removal and replacement of paper rolls. A dark blue background with a decorative border of contrasting light colors makes a good finish. We recommend sealing the acrylics on a project of this nature.

Modern Matchbox

The wall-hung matchbox was a common item in the colonial kitchen, and it still has more than a decorative purpose in today's home. Although less often used now than in days when wooden matches were a necessity in every home, the matchbox has a purpose beside the fireplace for holding either packs of safety matches or a larger box of the

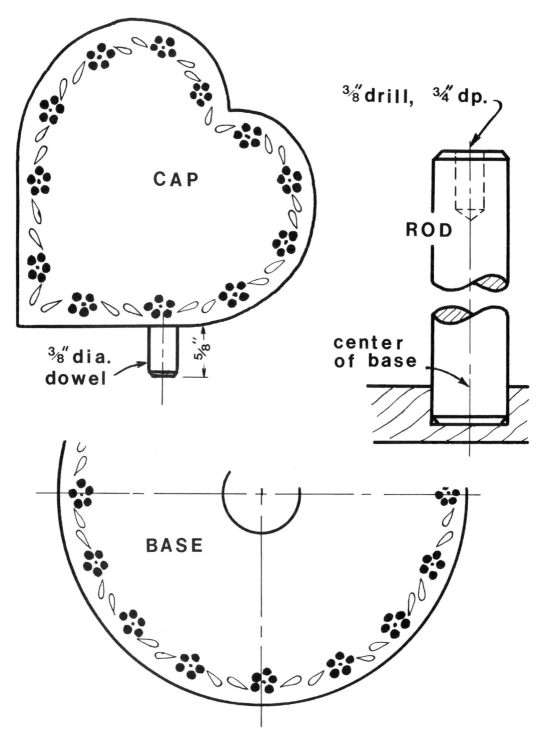

CAP

$\frac{3}{8}''$ drill, $\frac{3}{4}''$ dp.

ROD

$\frac{3}{8}''$ dia. dowel

$\frac{5}{8}''$

center of base

BASE

Fig. 8-6. Pattern, Towel Dispenser.

"strike-anywhere" type. The rapid repopularization of wood-burning space heaters has also brought on renewed interest in the kinds of accessories convenient for lighting a fire. Even in homes not so equipped the match box makes a handy place to keep small items.

The design in FIG. 8-7 will hold pens, pencils, or matches. It can easily be mounted on the wall, and it can be decorated to match any color scheme and decor.

Materials

$5/16"$ × $35/8"$ × $81/2"$ back
 piece
$5/16"$ × $35/8"$ × $35/8"$ × front
$5/16"$ × $21/16"$ × $35/8"$ × sides (2)
$5/16"$ × $21/16"$ × $3"$ bottom
woodworker's glue
$3/4"$ brads and wood filler
acrylics and sealer

Tools

scroll saw
hammer, vise, and nail set
sander and abrasive papers
drill and $3/16"$ diameter bit
artist's and $1/2"$ flat brushes

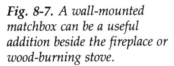

Fig. 8-7. A wall-mounted matchbox can be a useful addition beside the fireplace or wood-burning stove.

Refer to FIG. 8-8 for the pattern. This match box is designed for painting all over. Drive brads through the front and back pieces to hold the sides and through the front, back, and sides to hold the bottom insert in place.

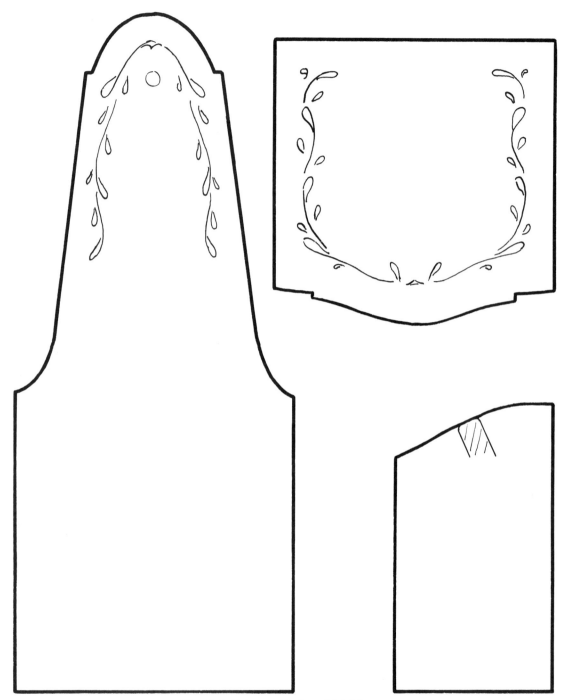

Fig. 8-8. Pattern, Modern Matchbox.

Add glue to the edges of the pieces before assembling to make the joints more secure. The setting of brads and leveling with filler proceeds in the normal way.

Sanding and painting complete the box, after drilling a $3/16$-inch hole for hanging the piece. Light yellow acrylic over a background of dark color, such as rust or colonial blue, makes the symmetrical design stand out effectively (FIG. 8-9). One or two spray coatings of matte sealer protect the acrylic while imparting a desirable appearance.

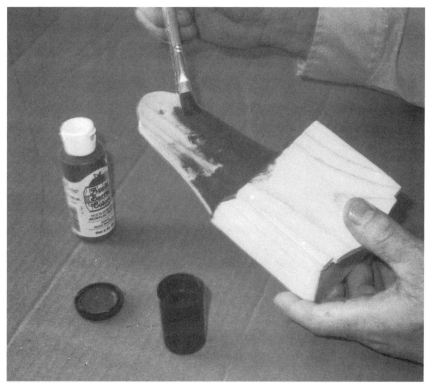

Fig. 8-9. Painting this assembly all over hides both the joints and the bradhole filler.

Kitty Cat Bookrack

Another useful and easily made project is this decorative bookrack (FIG. 8-10). The smoothly curved end pieces seem just right for a young girl's study area, and you need only three short dowel rods in between to support the books. Unlike unattached bookends, this assembly keeps the books in place without spreading apart.

Fig. 8-10. A customized bookrack makes a highly desirable addition to a child's room.

To add an individual touch, letter the user's name on an end piece. Paint or incise the lettering either on the inside or near the bottom on the outside of the piece. Young children like to see their names on things they own or use.

Materials	*Tools*
2 pcs., $3/4'' \times 7'' \times 10''$ knot free for the ends	scroll saw
	drill and $1/2''$ wood bit
3 dowel rods, $1/2''$ dia. $\times$ 12" long	sanding devices and abrasive paper
woodworker's glue	$1/2''$ flat and artist's brushes
assorted acrylics	paper

Refer to FIG. 8-11 for a pattern, and saw the end pieces to shape, keeping in mind that both will face the same direction. Sand the pieces overall (FIG. 8-12), mark locations on the insides for the three dowel rods, and drill $1/2$-inch-diameter holes about $9/16$ inch deep into each piece. Glue the ends of the rods into the drilled holes. If the fit is tight, you might have to drive the rods into the holes with a hammer after slightly beveling the tips. In any case, avoid loosely fitting rods, as they are not desirable in this project.

Lightly pencil or trace the design onto the wood, and apply acrylics of the desired colors. Finish the piece by coating it all over with one or two thin applications of satin polyurethane.

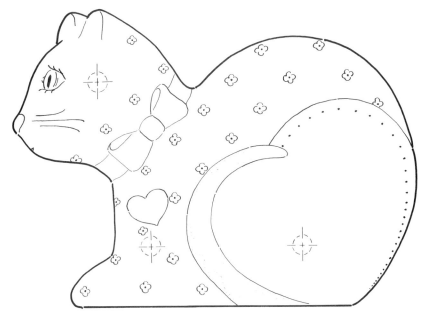

Fig. 8-11. Pattern, Kitty Cat Bookrack.

Fig. 8-12. A power sander often eases the chore of preparing a board's surfaces for painting.

9

Shelves, Seats, and Stools

Many artifacts brought forward from the time of settlement in America were made primarily for practical use. Decoration was generally omitted in the beginning, gaining prominence in the home as people became increasingly more affluent. Few settlers had time for unessentials. Most were too engrossed at the outset in the occupation of building a life in the country. Every family, parents and children alike, had to labor long and hard to satisfy the rudimentary needs of living.

The demands of establishing a homestead without much outside assistance left little room for creating the extras. Wood cleared from the land was fashioned into basic shelter and the necessities that went with it. Tables, benches, stools, troughs, and other household items were produced by hand and without much attention to matters other than use. Only occasionally was time found for less essential things, such as making toys for the children.

PRACTICAL PROCESSES

Today, pieces plainly designed in the manner of the early creations constitute a sizable portion of country art. Construction is often simple and traditional. Although you can use more advanced methods if you like, sometimes new applications for old forms are convenient.

The coffee table in FIG. 9-1 is an example. The design follows the general pattern of a wash bench, but it has been shortened and adorned

Fig. 9-1. Simple joinery, heart-shaped cutouts, and scalloped edges clearly show in this modern adapatation of a country bench.

with the familiar heart cutout. The buttons and joints impart an appearance of early work, and the dark stain coated with a non-glossy sealer produces the kind of complementary effect expected. Further, the use of pieces of one width has negated some sawing. This practice leaves the joints visible on the upper surface of the table—evidence of economical and unsophisticated construction. Modern methods would have the top extend over the sides to hide the joint.

To be consistent with tradition, the projects presented here are intended for assembly with an easily made kind of joint. We recommend using a simple butt joint, which accompanied the development of the nail, as opposed to forming the more complex blind, or hidden, mortise and tenon (FIG. 9-2). Figure 9-2C shows an acceptable construction, but this method of joinery requires extra care and close fitting for the glue to produce the necessary strength. The use of nails, as in FIG. 9-2A and 9-2B requires a bit of skill in camouflaging by setting the fasteners and covering their heads with tinted filler.

Shaker-Peg Shelf

Articles of wood are frequently based on designs once created by an uncommon sect, the Shakers, whose skill and craftsmanship has come to be admired in modern times. Wall-mounted shelves with Shaker pegs attached are highly prized today, even though the attachments might no

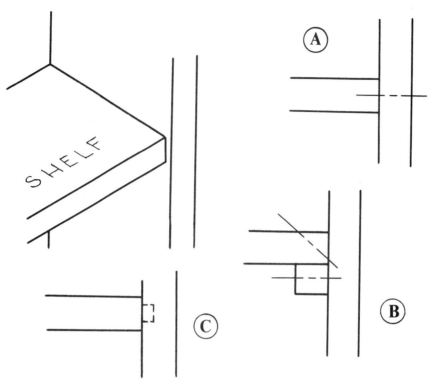

Fig. 9-2. Joint construction should meet the requirements of strength and appearance.

longer be intended for hanging hats and coats. The gracefully curved pieces are very popular, nevertheless, and wholesale quantities of the authentically formed pegs are readily available.

Figure 9-3 shows a shelf made with the mass-produced pegs. Scalloped edges in regular undulation and sawed out hearts symmetrically placed add to the quaintness of the piece. A further touch of magnificence from the past is a length of hand woven lace tacked along the shelf's edge.

Materials	Tools
3/4″ × 51/2″ × 60″ shelf board	jigsaw
3/4″ × 51/2″ × 591/2″ back board	drill and 1/2″ dia. bit
3/4″ × 4″ × 41/2″ brackets (2)	hammer and nail set
31/2″ Shaker pegs with	sander and abrasives
1/2″ dia. tenon (8)	brush and wiping cloth
6d finish nails and plastic wood	
woodworker's glue	
walnut stain, satin	
polyurethane, and thinner	

Fig. 9-3. *Shaker pegs and hand-made lace add effectively to this stained pine shelf.*

Because the layout can consume more time than the construction, consider the advantages of making a template for this article. Instead of making a drawing of the complete design (FIG. 9-4), cut pieces of thin cardboard (cereal boxes are good) in the shape of individual parts that occur repeatedly. Make one piece the shape of the brackets and another the contour of a section of the scalloped edge and a heart. Adjust the position of the template to suit when marking additional hearts on the wood.

Carefully saw and position the edges to eliminate the need for jointing or planing and to reduce the amount of sanding necessary. For example, the rough edge of a shelf board if faced toward the wall, does not need to be carefully finished because no one will see it.

Use either flathead screws or finishing nails for the assembly; evidence of such fasteners will be seen only from above or behind the shelf. Nails are entirely adequate if the boards are flat and the brackets fit snugly. Otherwise, wood screws will do a better job of pulling the joints tight. A thin covering of glue on the matching edges helps produce a more solid assembly.

The pattern for this article (FIG. 9-4), as is true of others in this section, contains only the curved parts. The convenience of having those details in readily usable form becomes apparent when preparing the layout. The original shelf was cut from the boards as dimensioned in the list of materials, but with some adjustment of the shapes, other sizes of shelves are producible in this or similar style.

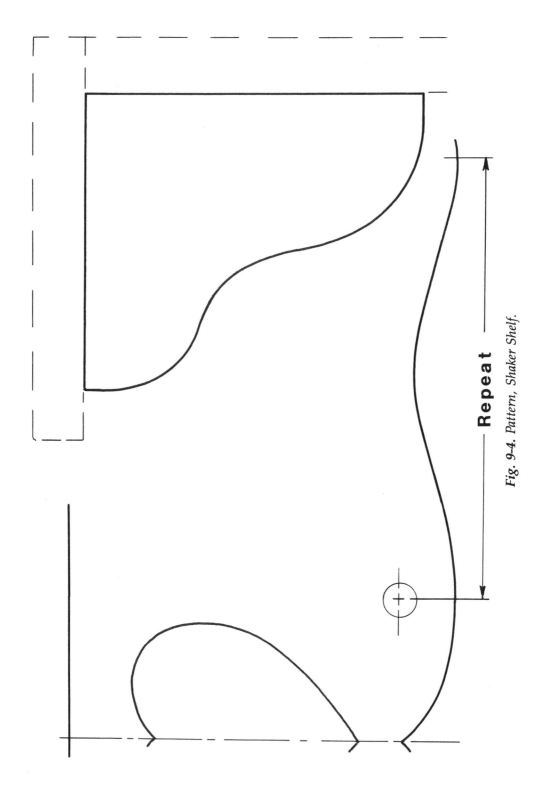

Fig. 9-4. Pattern, Shaker Shelf.

Sturdy Step Stool

An easily positioned, strong, stable stool is a handy item for reaching high places about the home. The one in FIG. 9-5 is made of solid pine and has a slot on top for gripping with one hand. The outward flare at the bottom provides a broad base of support, and the colorful hearts painted in a balanced arrangement on the sides and ends offset the stool's plainness.

Materials
1 1/8″ × 9 1/4″ × 11 1/4″ top piece
3/4″ × 8 3/4″ × 7 1/4″ ends (2)
3/4″ × 11 1/4″ × 7 1/4″ sides (2)
3/4 × 3/4″ × 6 3/4″ inside
  strips (2)
6d finishing nails and plastic wood
#10 FHB wood screws, 1 1/4″ long
woodworker's glue
acrylic paint, polyurethane,
  and mineral spirits

Tools
jigsaw and circular saw
drill, bits, and countersink
router with square and
  rounding bits
hammer and nail set
sander and abrasives
screwdriver
wood clamps
brushes, 1″ flat and assorted
  detailing

Fig. 9-5. A sturdy step stool is most convenient if designed to be lifted and carried with one hand.

Saw all pieces to size (FIG. 9-6), cutting the bottom and top edges of the side and end pieces on a 10-degree bevel. Bore two 1-inch diameter holes 2 3/4 inches, center to center, at the middle of the top, and remove the center section of the hand slot using a jig saw. Round all edges of the top piece, cut dados into the sides, and attach the 4-inch strips to the inside top of the sides using glue and screws. Assemble the sides and end

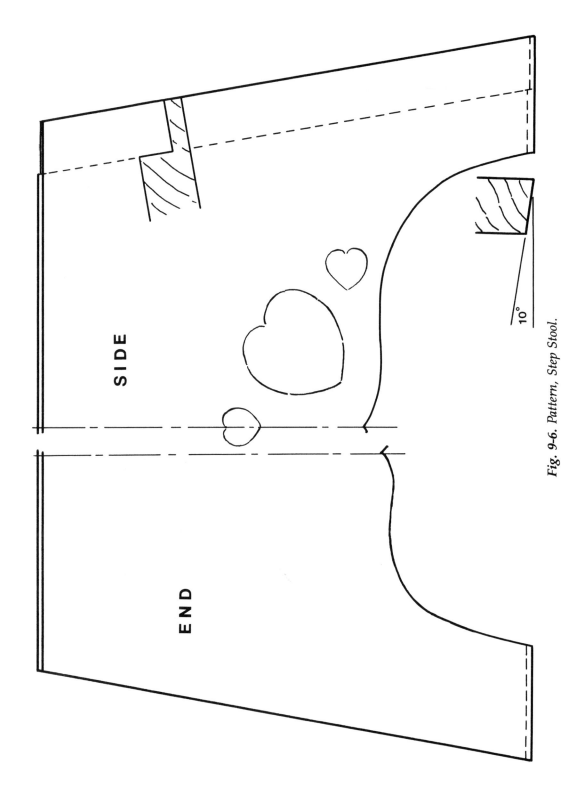

Fig. 9-6. Pattern, Step Stool.

SIDE

END

10°

pieces with glue and nails. Next, set and fill the nail holes. Machine-sand the outer surfaces before "blind" screwing the top in place. When assembled, finish the project by fine sanding, painting on the design, and applying polyurethane.

As an aid in painting, cut the several sizes of hearts from cardboard. Position the shapes where desired and trace around them with a soft-leaded pencil. After spotting all of the shapes, fill in the outlines using a red acrylic of slightly dark shade.

Sulker's Seat

The sulker's seat, or pouting chair as some know it, was a unique development. Once a disciplinary device for the ill-mannered child, it is used today as a decorative item. Although the originals were made for small youngsters and much in the style of the early potty-chair, most modern applications are made to a smaller scale for the purpose of holding stuffed toys upright. The reproductions are usually decorated as sparcely as the originals were.

A photograph of a chair made similar to an antique is presented in FIG. 9-7. The reproduction has been modified somewhat. Its smaller-than-original size makes it toy-like, and the tree of life, while a modernized version of a traditional symbol, effectively fills the symmetrically bounded area on the back.

Fig. 9-7. With a change in customs, the kind of chair once used in a child's discipline has gained popularity as a decorative item.

Materials

3/4" × 9¹/4" × 16¹/4" back piece
3/4" × 9¹/4" × 19" sides (2)
3/4" × 8" × 9¹/4" seat
3/4" × 3¹/4" × 9¹/4" apron
6d finishing nails and plastic
woodworker's glue
stain, polyurethane, and
    mineral spirits
acrylic paints, white and green

Tools

jigsaw and circular saw
hammer and nail set
sander and abrasives
wood clamps
1" flat brush and wiping cloth
artist's brushes and/or stencil
    brush

The lumber dimensions and large patterns we have provided (FIG. 9-8 and 9-9) eliminate much of the need for measuring and ripping boards to width. Using boards as they come from the mill in 10-inch widths, you only need to saw the large pieces to length before transferring and sawing the curved shapes. Moreover, few measurements are crucial in assembly.

Layout, sawing, sanding, edge gluing, and assembling follow ordinary procedures in woodworking. About the only process that is different is the painting of the decoration. Actually, you can use either of two procedures effectively: One is to stencil the design through a template, and the other is to outline the shapes with a pencil before painting in the shapes freehand. You might prefer the outline method, which doesn't require you to make a complete template. Paint the design on the stained wood before brushing on finish coats of polyurethane.

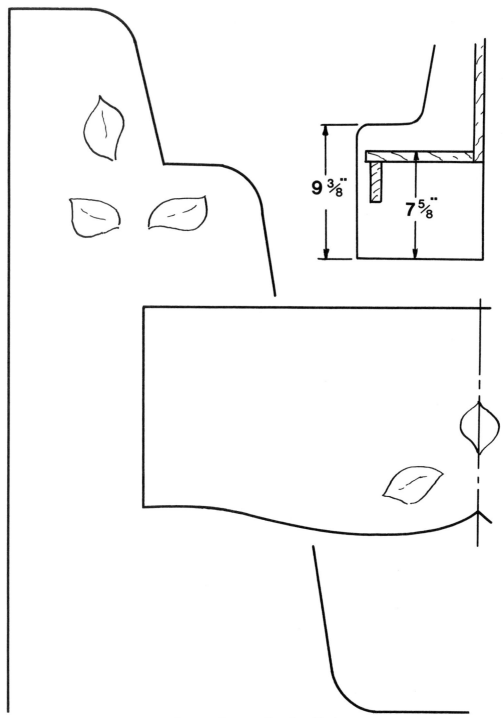

Fig. 9-8. Pattern, Pouting Chair.

Within the figure: **9 3/8″** and **7 5/8″**

Fig. 9-9. Pattern, Pouting Chair.

10
Making It Pay

Those who produce country creations on a regular basis need an outlet for their work. Dedicated professionals must be continually sustained by a buying public, but even the casual hobbyist needs to experience the reward of an occasional sale. An exception is the craftsman who does not tire of storing his work about the home and once in a while giving away a well-made piece.

If you are interested in making a business of your craft, whether full time or part time, you must market and sell what you make. Success in the undertaking requires more initiative and effort than talent. It also requires knowing which practices are effective, how to minimize the risks, and where to start. We have provided here some relevant suggestions and proven methods for a one- or two-person operation.

THE HOME ADVANTAGE

Probably the best approach for the beginner is to start in the home. Although there are other ways to build a successful operation, a home business offers the advantage of low risk. You need comparatively little operating capital, and you can start the complete operation on a part-time or weekend basis. Overhead is minimal, the time involved can be arranged as most fitting, and the dollar outlay is comparatively small. Even as your business grows and flourishes, you might find the cottage-industry method most effective and convenient.

Housewives, casual hobbyists, retirees, and entire families sometimes build and market their products at home. They do the work in spare hours and without loss of time commuting. They have the added advantage of managing the operation as they desire.

Having a workplace and an office in the home can be both boon and bane, however. On the one hand, you'll have tax breaks, and the convenient proximity of family members when they are needed. On the other hand, physical spaces (such as a corner of the garage for a shop and a bedroom for an office) are necessary (if not costly) provisions. Also, interruptions by friends and clients might be counterproductive unless you provide some control by attaching an answering machine to the telephone and establishing business hours. Despite the disadvantages, the cottage-industry approach is ideal for establishing a business of this kind, especially for making and selling the crafts in limited quantities.

PRACTICAL PROCEDURES

Knowledge of certain practical procedures becomes essential when producing and marketing crafts in and from the home. You'll need to learn efficient methods of constructing, distributing, and selling the items. Also, you must comply with zoning and licensing requirements.

As your business undergoes gradual expansion, or when the holiday rush season nears, it will become more important to do your craftwork quickly. One way is to shape and assemble a large quantity of objects and do all the painting at one sitting. A second practical consideration is to saw out duplicates, or stacks, of wooden parts in a single operation. One successful housewife not only does this but also carries the method a step further by having her young sons do the sanding in assembly-line fashion. Be sure when you simplify procedures and use time-saving methods that you maintain the same level of quality as if the pieces were carefully made one-of-a-kind. The results will ultimately affect sales.

For selling to be successful over the long pull, you should always give the customer a product of the same quality observed in the display model. That is what the buyer has come to expect. While some country crafts are intentionally rough or folkish, and others are properly given a more highly refined and finished appearance, a client who pays for one thing but receives a product that seems cheaper will probably not buy another nor be a good spokesperson for the business. Failure to deal honestly and fairly with clients will almost certainly lead to failure of the business.

Marketing directly to the customer, as we recommend for small businesses of this kind, requires you to keep a variety of samples on hand. You should select and retain models for showing that have appeal, displaying both decorative and utilitarian items. When it's not possible or desirable to keep duplicates of all the products, put together color photographs of the missing pieces in an attractive binder for your customers to peruse.

In the beginning, try to visit gift shops and attend craft shows to see what the competition is marketing. By observing what people are buying, as opposed to concentrating on all that is being displayed, you can make versions of slightly different design. Over time, you'll be able to tell precisely what sells well and what doesn't.

Always give prospective buyers the attention they want, even if it means interrupting important shop work. Also, allow them to "customize" a product of their choice by specifying the colors to be used. Doing these things might involve extra effort, but sooner or later the extra consideration will pay dividends.

The practical aspects of marketing and selling are important, and their application will go a long way toward building a successful business. By establishing a reputation for fairness and giving customers what they want, word-of-mouth advertising could soon outdo all of the distributions of printed literature used to promote the business.

SUPPLYING THE SKILLS

The building of a successful home business depends on providing skills common to the craftsman, artisan, marketing specialist, salesperson, accountant, and legal authority. Fortunately, a high degree of expertise is not needed in each area of concern, nor are lengthy apprenticeships and a degree in business administration prerequisites. The skills ordinarily required are within the ability of those who take the time to become reasonably well-informed. Unfortunately, by most standards, few people inform themselves fully before starting, and seldom do they seek professional advice on matters not within their grasp. The costs are often believed to be too great for an operation having limited capital and an uncertain future.

What most people do have at the beginning is skill in producing and designing their crafts. Marketing and selling skills are then developed in an amateurish, trial-and-error manner, often by trying one thing after another as observed in use by others. The legal and financial requirements also seem to be heaped onto the workload much in the random order in which they occur. Solid planning seems to be missing. If you want to avoid serious difficulties, the suggestions given below should be viewed as a minimum for entering this sometimes bewildering arena.

PRICING AND PROMOTING

The difficult question of how much to charge for country creations might be answered, in part, by this formula:

Price = Operating + Cost of + Labor & + Profit
         Overhead   Material   Benefts

Compute the price for an item from the many factors representing the cost of producing the goods plus an amount needed to stay in business. You'll find that much depends on your circumstances. For example, if you work at home, you might figure a portion of utility bills and expenses for the family automobile into your business costs. By way of contrast, you would charge tools and material purchased exclusively for the business fully to that account. One rule holds for all such expenses: **Only that portion used in the business may be expensed to it**.

Labor and taxes might be significant costs to consider. If someone assists you in the shop, you need to consider wages and fringe benefits and reduce them to calculations on an item-by-item basis. Social security and other taxes might require similar treatment.

As for profit, we advise beginners to settle for a reasonable wage at first. Concentrate on establishing a good reputation with the idea in mind of increasing the profit margin as the demand and backlog of orders grow. One person who followed that practice was able to increase prices six times over the initial charge in a period of four years.

The amount competitors charge might also serve as a guide to pricing, but be careful because some low quality, mass-produced pieces, including items made in foreign countries, are flooding the market. The profit margin and, hence, the total price for handcrafted pieces might range widely according to the interests and financial status of the clientele. In addition, the demand in the market generally and the effectiveness of promotional efforts make a difference.

The business must be promoted on a timely basis. Unless you do this at the outset, you can expect little success. Well-designed business cards, which include a catchy name or title for the operation, and one-page flyers showing the location and directions can be very valuable. You can distribute these with each purchase at the home and to the general public at local arts and crafts shows. Mail flyers with gift suggestions to likely customers who live within easy traveling distance. Suggestions mailed in time for the holidays are often most effective.

Because mailing can be a very expensive way to advertise, "test the water" by selectively mailing literature to potential customers other than established clientele. Newspapers can be helpful in this regard. Mothers of young ladies whose engagements or forthcoming weddings are announced in local dailies and weeklies are logical prospects for buying gifts for the new household. Each such mother who receives the mailing will then know where attractive handcrafted items can be bought for herself or for someone else, even if she does not buy something immediately for her daughter. Very likely, this technique will prove to be far more beneficial than trying to sell the crafts through expensive newspaper ads.

Word-of-mouth promotion is best of all over the long haul. Nothing is more effective than having a satisfied customer spread the word. That's why it is so important to build a reputation for quality and reasonable pricing at the outset and to make the existence of the business known throughout the surrounding area. Displaying items in consignment shops and at handcraft shows will give the business some visibility, but that practice is seldom as productive as it is costly. For selling country crafts, the house party is a better way to go.

HAVING A PARTY

Several of the techniques used in the business world work very effectively in the marketing and selling of tangible, homemade goods. Nationally known companies, specifically those involved in marketing directly to households, teach their salespeople to set up group demonstrations in the home of a willing and enthusiastic client. Rather than have their representatives display goods before one housewife or family, they suggest having someone schedule a party of a dozen or so friends and neighbors. These businesses usually offer a gift to the person who brings the group together for the presentation. Additionally, the salespeople are taught to obtain leads of prospects from those who buy something.

Items handcrafted in the country style are ideal for selling by this method. The investment in a few gifts (country creations, by all means) and incidentals for the house parties, such as cookies and coffee, can return many times over.

You might also consider varying the value of gifts for hostesses according to the benefits received, especially according to the dollar volume of purchases by those present at the shows. We have had a great deal of success ourselves by printing a schedule on the back sheet of our catalog. For hosting a house party, the gift is a small candle holder; for total sales over $100, the choice of a welcome sign; over $250, a decorative heart or 18-inch shelf; and, over $500, the choice of any catalog item. Our stated willingness to contribute a percentage to charity also seems to be a very effective incentive.

The house party has considerable advantages because the hostess does much of the preliminary work. She will identify and invite all attendees, inform them of the purpose of the meeting, provide the place for the presentation, serve the amenities (which you supply or pay for), and help in leading the small talk as a way of relieving the guest's tensions and initial anxieties. The likelihood of her inviting friends and acquaintances also helps to "break the ice," but it has the added advantage for you in that a sale to one of the group is usually not allowed to go unmatched or unsurpassed by the others as it might among complete strangers. The psychology involved can be a powerful stimulus. The first sale might be slow in coming, but once it occurs other orders usually follow.

Don't overlook the importance of asking the hostess to invite people she thinks will be interested in buying the crafts. For example, guests known to be "tight" with the dollar could be both poor customers and bad influences. A good hostess, if offered an extra or larger gift based on the volume of sales, will not only prescreen her list of invitees but will probably help promote sales.

Although a sales party can be held at almost any time of the year, the holiday seasons are best. People are then in a buying mood and have laid away savings for gifts of all kinds, both essential and luxurious. The days shortly after Thanksgiving are particularly good.

Plan to hold such parties during the evening on weekdays or in the afternoon of weekends. People can more easily arrange to attend then.

The room used for the presentation should contain comfortable seating and a place for displaying various pieces. Some items, such as wall plaques, brooches, and small shelves, might be more visible to all if you mounted them on one or more peg boards with supports. Try to show pieces large and small, expensive and inexpensive, functional and decorative, and of considerable variety. Everything should be in place before the guests arrive, leaving you free to greet everyone as they arrive.

Immediately before a presentation, seat yourself with the guests and engage in casual conversation. The idea is to create a friendly atmosphere and build rapport. One need not drink coffee or eat cookies to show genuine interest in the people present. Do not smoke at any time, regardless of what the guests do.

Start the meeting as close to the scheduled time as possible. Have the hostess prepared to reintroduce you and to restate the purpose of the gathering. If she is familiar with your work and likes it, she might even give it a helpful unsolicited plug.

Stand squarely before the group during the talk. Look into their eyes when speaking, and show enthusiasm for your work. Explain what, why, and how your crafts are good for them. Emphasize the benefits of ownership.

In the discussion of a wall shelf, for example, you might say something like this: "Here's a shelf that is both useful and attractive. It has an authentic country styling, and you can have it done in colors to match your own decor. It is excellent for displaying bric-a-brac in the hallway or dining room where guests will see it and surely comment about it. It can also be used for holding spice jars in the kitchen. It is handcrafted and stenciled—the kind of thing your children and grandchildren might want to enjoy and keep passing down the family chain. Perhaps, like many handmade things, it will continue to increase in value as time goes by.

"By the way, my neighbor saw a piece much like this one in my home. Her lavish comments about its beauty were quite flattering. It is attractive, though, isn't it?

"You can have one like it, or in a size and decorative color of your choice. Make a note of it for reference after I have shown you other selections you can use in your home or give as gifts."

Selling requires imagination. It is the process of removing barriers and presenting reasons for ownership so that the customer actually wants to make the purchase. Try to make occasional reference to comments made by a satisfied customer. The testimony of a third party will sometimes be the clincher you need.

Also try to start the demonstration with an expensive item. Things shown thereafter will then seem more affordable. Have the price written on a small stick-on slip attached to the item's bottom or backside. Then you will not have to commit such facts to memory, and the buyers will know you have settled on a price beforehand.

TAKING ORDERS AND KEEPING TRACK

During the presentation, involve the group by seeking comments from individuals, and observe closely how each responds to questions. Ask simple things, such as what one likes about a particular item. That process helps condition individuals to feeling and speaking positively about the different things being shown. Another idea is to identify a person who seems likely to be a large buyer and the one to call upon first when taking orders after all pieces have been shown. This selection can be extremely important, for others tend to follow the lead purchase.

Give each person an opportunity to place an order, and try to get everyone present to make a purchase. Pass your photo album to any who hesitate, suggesting that something shown in it might be more suitable for him or her.

When all ordering has been done, or has reached a lull, present the hostess's gift to her. If conditions warrant it, you might want to tell the group that their hostess will receive a bonus gift if a couple people add to their orders. People are usually willing to help their friends, so you might get a few extra orders this way. Always make a positive display of the gift. If nothing else, it will show the others how rewarding being hostess can be.

Record every item on a regular sales slip. Include the purchaser's name, phone number and address, the price of each item, the total cost, and the tax, if any. The sales slip should also show the amount of payment received and the balance due. Give a duplicate copy to the buyer. Keep a copy as a permanent record for filling the order and for future mailings.

Try to be prompt in filling each order. Ideally, you should deliver each item in person or have the buyer stop by your house to pick it up so you can use the occasion to suggest additional items, such as gifts for someone who might have been overlooked. Then, too, if the person seems right for it, determine her interest in hosting a house party of her own. She might be the very one you want to set up your next sale presentation.

As to records, be accurate and complete. Record everything that pertains to the business. A neat, precise, easily understood, daily listing of expenses and receipts is essential. Employ an accountant when the business becomes large or the bookkeeping seems too complicated.

You must also take into account certain legal matters. One is to obtain proper identification from the Internal Revenue Service for the payment of social security tax. In addition, check with state and local authorities about sales taxes and any restrictions for operating the business from your home. By taking these basic precautions at the outset, you can avoid serious problems at a later time.

Index

A

acorn miniature figures, 35
acrylic paints, 7, 11, 15-17
adhesives and glues, 12
Amish people cutout figures, 28-30
angel miniature figures, 37
apple miniature figures, 35
assembled (multi-part) figures, 42-51
    adhesives and glues, 42
    big-eared bunny, 49-51
    cutting, 43
    duck candleholder, 47-49
    finishes, 44
    sanding, 43
    screws or doweling, 44
    shaping pieces for assembly, 42
    weathercock figure, 44-46
assembly steps, 42-44

B

basket holder teddy bear, 26-28
bears (see teddy bears)
bird miniature figures, 37
bookracks, cat design, 87-89
buildings, miniature figures, 38-41

C

candleholders
    cat, 36
    duck, 47-49
cats
    bookrack, 87-89
    candleholder, 36
    Cat and Dog Couple comical characters, 74-78
    cutout figure, 25
    Fat Cat comical characters, 73-74
    miniature figures, 35, 37
chickens
    cutout figures, 22-25
    rowdy roosters plaque, mottos and messages, 59-63
    weathercock figure, 44-46
    You Do It comical characters, 67-69
Christmas decorations, mottos and messages, 53
coffee table, 90-91
comical characters, 64-78
    captions, 64
    caricature creation, 64-65
    Cat and Dog couple, 74-78
    Fat Cat, 73-74
    Munching Mouse, 70-73
    You Do It chicken, 67-69
cutout figures, 18-30
    Amish couples, 28-30
    cat figure, 25
    chicken couples, 22-25
    finishing, 18
    goose couples, 22-25
    pattern transfer procedures, 18
    rocking horse figure, 20-22
    sanding, 18-19
    sawing and cutting, 18-19
    sheep couples, 22-25
    teddy bear basket holder, 26-28
    wood selection, 18

D

design principles, 1-6, 102
    American historical designs, background and development, 1-2
    decorative vs. functional design, 3-5, 79-80, 90-91
    developing individual designs, 5-6
    rough-in drawing, 66
dogs, Cat and Dog Couple comical characters, 74-78
doweling, 12

drills, 11
ducks
  candleholder, 47-49
  miniature figures, 35, 37

F

finishes, 11, 15-17
flour sack miniature figures,
  35
flowers, tulip miniature
  figures, 35

G

geese
  cutout figures, 22-25
  welcome plaque, 56-58
glues and adhesives, 12

H

hangers and hooks, 12-13
hearts
  coffee table, 90-91
  hearts-and-doves welcome
    plaque, 58-60
  miniature figures, 35
  paper towel dispenser, 82-84
  Shaker-peg shelf, 3, 91-94
  step stool, 95-97
hearts-and-doves welcome
  plaque, 58-60
hooks and hangers, 12-13
horses, rocking horse cutout,
  20-22
household objects, 79-89
  bookrack, cat design, 87-89
  decorative vs. functional
    design, 79-80
  felt pads on bottom, 82
  finishes and paints, 80-81
  matchbox, 83-87
  napkin holder, 80
  paper towel dispenser, 82-84
  template construction, 81

L

lettering, 14-15, 55-56

M

magnetic stick-ups (*see*
  miniature figures)
matchbox, 83-87

materials, 8, 10-12
mice, Munchin Mouse comical
  characters, 70-73
miniature figures, 31-41
  acorns, 35
  adhesives and glues, 32-33
  angel, 37
  apple, 35
  bears, 38-41
  bird, 37
  buildings, 38-41
  bunnies, 38-41
  candleholders, 36
  cat, 35, 37
  cords and clasps
    attachment, 32
  duck, 35, 37
  finishes, 32-33
  flour sacks, 35
  hearts, 35
  magnet attachment, 32-33
  materials selection, 32
  pattern reduction, 31-32
  pig, 35
  pineapple, 35
  rub-on transfers, 32-33
  sheep, 35
  soldier, 37
  tulip, 35
  watermelon slice, 35
mottos and messages, 52-63
  Christmas decorations, 53
  decorative border designs,
    54
  goose-shaped welcome
    plaque, 56-58
  hearts-and-doves welcome
    plaque, 58-60
  rowdy roosters plaque,
    59-63
  sample slogans, 52-54
  stenciling letters, 55-56
  wall plaque design, 54-55
  wall plaque welcome, 53

N

napkin holder, 80

P

paints, 7, 11, 15-17

paper towel dispenser, 82-84
pattern enlargement,
  reduction, 7-10
pig miniature figure, 35
pineapple miniature figures,
  35
pins (*see* miniature figures)
  quilt-cleaning figurine, 4

R

rabbits
  assembled (multi-part)
    figures, 49-51
  figurine, 5
  miniature figures, 38-41
rocking horse cutout, 20-22
rowdy roosters plaque, 59-63
rub-on transfers, 32-33

S

sanding, 11
saws, 8, 10
sealers, 16-17
seats and stools, 90-100
  coffee table, 90-91
  practical and functional
    designs, 90
  step stool, 95-97
  sulker's seat, 97-100
selling handcrafts, 101-108
  direct marketing, 102-103
  inventories, 102, 107-108
  materials, 102
  order-taking, 107-108
  party selling, 105-107
  pricing and promotion,
    103-106
  selection, 102
  shows and fairs, 102
  skill development, 103
  taxes, 104, 108
  templates and duplicates,
    102
  time vs. cost, 103-104
Shaker-peg shelf, 3, 91-94
sheep
  cutout figures, 22-25
  miniature figures, 35
shelves, 90-100

practical and functional designs, 90
   Shaker-peg shelf, 3, 91-94
soldier miniature figures, 37
stains, 15-17
stenciling, 3, 14-15, 55-56
step stool, 95-97
stools (*see* seats and stools)
sulker's seat, 97-100

T

taxes, 104, 108
teddy bears
   basket holder, 26-28
   miniature figures, 38-41
template construction, 8, 10, 81
tools, 8, 10-12
transfers, rub-on, 32-33

W

wall plaque welcome mottos and messages, 53
watermelon slice miniature figures, 35
weathercock figure, 44-46
welcome plaques (*see* mottos and messages)
wood selection, 11-12

Other Bestsellers of Related Interest

ONE-WEEKEND COUNTRY FURNITURE PROJECTS—Percy W. Blandford

Transform simple materials into beautiful, functional objects with this brand-new selection of original projects to use in and around your home, in an easy, one-weekend format, especially for time-conscious hobbyists. A basic understanding of woodworking techniques is all you need to build an attractive, durable piece of furniture in as little as 12 hours. You get nearly 50 original project plans—all requiring only simple hand tools and inexpensive materials—and ample drawings and instructions for every design. 240 pages, 163 illustrations. Book No. 3702, $14.95 paperback, $24.95 hardcover

KATHY LAMANCUSA'S GUIDE TO WREATH MAKING—Kathy Lamancusa, C.P.D.

Now, you can enjoy the inviting charm of handcrafted wreaths in your home all year long. Lamancusa clearly explains the most intricate aspects of wreath making. Beginning with the basics, you'll look at the materials used in wreath making with instructions for locating, cutting, and combining them. Then you'll move on to such projects as bows, kitchen wreaths, seasonal wreaths, wreaths for children, romantic wreaths, masculine wreaths, special occasion wreaths. 128 pages, 133 illustrations. Book No. 3492, $10.95 paperback, $19.95 hardcover

KATHY LAMANCUSA'S GUIDE TO FLORAL DESIGN—Kathy Lamancusa, C.P.D.

Create exquisite silk and dried floral designs for *every* room of your home with this easy-to-follow guide. You'll learn to work with the various materials and supplies and master basic design techniques quickly and easily with step-by-step photographs and instructions. Then you'll go beyond the legendary techniques to create fresher, more modern styles. Projects include wall and table arrangements, baskets, and special occasion designs. 128 pages, 166 illustrations. Book No. 3491, $12.95 paperback, $21.95 hardcover

THE DRILL PRESS BOOK: Including 80 Jigs and Accessories to Make—R. J. De Cristoforo

The drill press, after the table saw, is the second most important tool in the workshop. In this well-illustrated guide, you'll discover unique ways to develop the tool's potential in over 80 project plans. As De Cristoforo guides you through each application of this versatile tool, you'll benefit from hundreds of hints based on his years of woodworking experience. 304 pages, 406 illustrations. Book No. 3609, $16.95 paperback, $25.95 hardcover

CRAFTS FOR KIDS: A Month-By-Month Idea Book —2nd Edition—Barbara L. Dondiego

Illustrations by Jacqueline Cawley

Packed with dozens of project ideas, this collection of simple and inexpensive crafts is great for teaching children ages, preschool through elementary, about colors, shapes, numbers, and letters, as well as aiding them in their development of hand-eye coordination and motor skills. This revised edition features 20 all-new projects, including crafts for all major holidays, gift-giving, and cooking crafts. 240 pages, 164 illustrations. Book No. 3573, $14.95 paperback only

DESIGNING AND CONSTRUCTING MOBILES —Jack Wiley

Discover the fun and satisfaction of learning to create exciting mobile art forms . . . to add a personal decorator touch to your home, as unique craft projects for school class or club, even as a new income source! All the skills and techniques are here for the taking in this excellent, step-by-step guide to designing and constructing mobiles from paper, wood, metals, plastic, and other materials. 224 pages, 281 illustrations. Book No. 1839, $19.95 hardcover only

FRAMES AND FRAMING: The Ultimate Illustrated How-to-Do-It Guide—Gerald F. Laird and Louise Meière Dunn, CPF

This illustrated step-by-step guide gives complete instructions and helpful illustrations on how to cut mats, choose materials, and achieve attractively framed art. Filled with photographs and eight pages of full color, this book shows why a frame's purpose is to enhance, support, and protect the artwork, and never call attention to itself. You can learn how to make a beautiful frame that complements artwork. 208 pages, 264 illustrations. Book No. 2909, $13.95 paperback only

MAKING POTPOURRI, COLOGNES AND SOAPS: 102 Natural Recipes—David A. Webb

Fill your home with the scents of spring—all year long! This down-to-earth guide reintroduces the almost forgotten art of home crafts. You'll learn how to use simple ingredients (flowers, fruits, spices, and herbs) to make a variety of useful scented products, from soaps and deodorant to potpourris and colognes. Webb demystifies this age-old craft and offers step-by-step diagrams, work-in-progress photographs, and easy-to-follow recipes to give you everything you need to create your own home crafts. 144 pages, 98 illustrations. Book No. 2918, $9.95 paperback, $18.95 hardcover